CONTENTS

To my family:

past, present, and future;

nuclear and extended;

especially Vida, John-Thomas, and James Weldon

TEACHING SCRIPTURE
from an
AFRICAN-AMERICAN
PERSPECTIVE

Joseph V. Crockett

DISCIPLESHIP RESOURCES
MATERIALS FOR GROWTH IN CHRISTIAN FAITH AND LIFE
P.O. Box 189 • Nashville, TN 37202 • Phone (615) 340-7284

Revised 1991.

Unless otherwise noted, all scripture quotations are from the New Revised Standard Version of the Holy Bible, copyright © 1989 by the Division of Christian Education of the National Council of the Churches of Christ in the United States of America. Used by permission.

Library of Congress Card Catalog No. 90-82978

ISBN 0-88177-086-8

DR086B

FOREWORD

Amerian society, particularly the church, has long needed a book that would give careful attention to the Christian education of African Americans. The long history of oral tradition in the African-American church has rich values, many of which have been only lately addressed and made clear. Books on Black theology, while important as a group, often failed to address the important place that the Bible has played—and can play—in the Christian education of a group of people with a peculiar history.

Joseph V. Crockett has met the church's need in a splendid way. Carefully outlining four basic themes in African-American Christian education, he goes on to show how these themes can tell a people's particular story within the broad context of the biblical story. His book is a basic contribution to the understanding of African-American cultural history and tradition around themes of story, exile, sanctuary, and exodus.

This book will be of great value to those who plan for and teach in African-American churches. It will also be helpful to those who want to understand the treasure of faith that is yet to be discovered in churches with a peculiarly rich folk knowledge of the biblical story.

JAMES S. THOMAS, BISHOP
THE UNITED METHODIST CHURCH

PREFACE

The study of scripture, educational strategies, and African-American culture raises many questions. These questions include, What are the educational processes that can communicate the church's beliefs and traditions? What processes allow persons unfamiliar with the church's tradition to learn, critique, revise, and claim that tradition? What is the church's tradition that is to be transmitted and discovered? What is the African-American heritage that is to be communicated and explored? How are two kinds of content, the biblical and the African-American, to be used in matters of interpretation? When is the biblical narrative to govern the African-American narrative? When and how do the history and culture of African Americans critique the biblical interpretations of the church? And why is the name African American rather than Afro-American, Black, or Negro used to refer to the group of persons that is the subject of discussion? Two questions are taken up immediately, and the others will be discussed throughout this book.

The term *African American* gives primary attention to the anthropological journey of Black Americans. *African American* as a term refers to the geographical origin of the Black race. Members of the Black race may live on the continental shores of the Americas, in Europe, or in other locations. But our roots are located in the soil of Africa.

The term *African American* also refers to the particular nation under which a segment of the Black race claims civil allegiance, with the nation of a civil allegiance being the United States of America. Use of the term *African American* in this manner makes it possible to discuss both a commonality and a distinctive characteristic of African Americans with all people.

When hyphenated, the term is used as an adjective to make specific the noun that follows. For example, "African-American congregations" suggests congregations with a particular history and tradition.

Concerning questions about principles of interpretation, the issues are more intricate. One reason is that issues of interpretation involve the interpreter's view of reality. Perception, the act of collecting objects within one's realm of awareness, is forever a discriminating experience. Consciously, subconsciously, and unconsciously, individuals choose to give attention to some phenomena while they do not apprehend other phenomena. For example, European Americans used the letter of Paul to the Ephesians (6:9) to support the institution and practices of slavery. African-American slaves fought against institutions of slavery supported by the same author's writings to the Colossians (3:11).

How, then, are two kinds of content, biblical and the African-American, to be used in matters of interpretation? When is the biblical narrative to govern a historical-cultural narrative and vice versa? First, the biblical and African-American experiences are distinguishable, but not separable. The God of eternity is also the God of all history. God is not bound to one particular people, place, or time. Israel, the early church, and African Americans—all are related to God.

Second, as learners approach the task of interpretation, they must do so with openness, abandoning "fixed" and preconceived views about God's activity. The experiences of Judeo-Christians and the experiences of African Americans happen in God. Neither the biblical nor the African-American experiences alone exhaust God's reality. God's being and ways are responsive to the actions of both, but are not limited to either. The process of interpretation does not need to exclude one experience at the expense of validating the other. While the inclusion of both the biblical and African-American experiences may not result in their synthesis, it can result in each being critiqued and revised.

Finally, biblical interpretation involves the weighing of scripture in relation to African Americans' personal and communal feelings, thoughts, and life tasks. Persons learn who they are and who they may become in relation to others. They gain a sense of what to do and what to hold as important by giving attention to the authority of scripture, reason, and the church's tradition. But the references that help define one's sense of self and purpose can also lead to a negation of personal and communal experience.

Processes of interpretation can become one-sided. When learners seek only the opinions and views of others—the church, the tradition, the pastor, or the teacher—their own biographical and cultural history is invalidated. What is recorded in scripture contributes to a culture's views, feelings, sense of identity, and vocation. Likewise, the experiences of a people add to their interpretation of the Bible. Interpreting scripture must show coherence within the biblical witness, and the interpretation must address adequately the African-American context.

The processes of interpretation regarding scripture and African-American culture focus clearly two underlying concerns of this book. Namely, what is the content of the church that is to be passed on? And what are the processes for handing the content on to culture-specific communities? Both issues are rooted in understandings of tradition—the content to be transmitted *(traditia)* and the processes of transmitting *(traditio)*. The questions below may be of additional help in the task of interpretation.

1. Does the interpretation invite the biblical and African-American experiences to be trusted?

2. Does the interpretation of scripture have power to address the needs, problems, and concerns of African Americans?

3. Does the interpretation of scripture make sense of the African-American experience without denying the experience or destroying the humanness of African Americans?

4. Does the interpretation help African Americans strengthen cultural identity and enhance connectedness with the human community?

ACKNOWLEDGMENTS

Many persons helped in the development and testing of the strategies of education of African-American congregations. The steering committee, composed of Carolyn Anderson, Ethel Johnson, Grant S. Shockley, H. Walter Willis, Jr., and Fred D. Smith provided valuable insight regarding the identification of the issues and approaches. In addition to her work as a committee member, Ethel Johnson gave encouragement and support when the clouds of unknowing were at their zenith.

Ten churches and annual conferences of The United Methodist Church were invited to use two or more of the educational strategies as part of their program of education. Without apology they provided for me a reality check. Persons who participated include Sharon Adair, Ronald T. Brown, Richard (Dick) Brunner, Via Clay, Bettye Corcoran, Sandy Ferguson, Joyce Favors, Betty A. Henderson, Grant Johnson, Vaughn A. Johnson, JoAnn Lawson, Helen J. Owens, Joyce Paldino, and Liz St. Clair.

Colleagues in agencies and institutions of The United Methodist Church gave freely of their expertise and experience. Anne and Ed Wimberly gave encouragement and confirmation to the work on the story strategy of education. Duane A. Ewers, Charles Foster, Nellie Moser, Jack L. Seymour, and Judy Smith are worthy of special mention. Their loyalty to the teaching ministry of the church, their undying commitment to issues of inclusiveness, and their expertise in education and editing have contributed much to the character of the final manuscript. Cecile A. Beam and Angela Gay Kinkead helped me clarify concepts, put flesh on abstractions, and use words that all would understand.

Appreciation goes to the students at The Methodist Theological School in Delaware, Ohio, the Divinity School of Vanderbilt University, and Garrett-Evangelical Theological Seminary, who learned with and taught me as we explored issues of Christian education in African-American congregations. These students judged gently, clarified compassionately, and offered many practical insights about how things "really" are in the church.

Gratitude is extended to my administrator, Marilyn W. Magee, and to the editorial and support staff of the General Board of Discipleship. Joyce Shepler and Nadina Wooding perfected their research, editing, and typing skills. And David Hazlewood and Craig Gallaway met, consulted, and gave helpful insights that make for a better reading and understanding of the manuscript.

A personal word of thanks to Vida, my wife, and "Daddy James," family members who have nurtured and continue to nurture me along the way.

INTRODUCTION

This book is about scripture and hearing the voice and discovering the movement of God. It is about God's dance in history made known to the church through the record of the Old and New Testaments. This book is about God's presence continuing to be made known to humanity from John's Revelation to the present. It is about the responses of humans, as individuals and communities, to God's presence and activity in the world.

This book is about understanding the Bible as the Word of God—the Word that is the primary text of the Christian community. It is about seeing the Old and New Testaments as pillars of faith that seek understanding and that give definition to the church's character and purpose. This book is about the letters that contain the Christian community's legacy of faith. It is about the Bible, the church's caldron that holds its memory and language, its heritage and hope. This book is about discovering and exploring the Holy Bible with generations of Christians yet unborn.

This book is about teaching. It is about teachers and learners with a peculiar history. Its educational aim is to influence five aspects of the teaching/learning experience. The book hopes to inspire teachers and learners with courage to study scripture. Persons will become moved and interested in disciplines of learning. This book aims to help teachers and learners identify concerns that long for their responses. Learners and teachers will be led to give attention to the thoughts of their hearts. The book is written to enable teachers and learners to acquire knowledge about the Bible. Teachers and learners will become able to discover, recall, and remember the names, events, purposes, and meanings of scripture. Learners and teachers will be empowered to reconstruct understandings by integrating particular experiences and the Word of God. They will be encouraged to use the knowledge gained in day-to-day life.

This book is about African-American communities of Christians. These communities are diverse. They are not static, but are continually changing. Many persons are unaware of the significant resources of African-American communities. Paul Laurence Dunbar may have reasoned correctly about why African-American resources and capabilities are largely unknown. In his poem, "We Wear the Mask," Dunbar wrote,

> We wear the mask that grins and lies,
> It hides our cheeks and shades our eyes,
> This debt we pay to human guile;
> With torn and bleeding hearts we smile,
> And mouth with myriad subtleties.
> Why should the world be overwise,
> In counting all our tears and sighs?
> Nay, let them only see us, while
> We wear the mask.
>
> We smile, but, O great Christ, our cries
> To Thee from tortured souls arise.
> We sing, but oh, the clay is vile
> Beneath our feet, and long the mile;
> But let the world dream otherwise,
>   We wear the mask.[1]

African Americans have a heritage rich with the rhythms of heroines and heroes. We have a soul born in the bosom of African soil that has laughed through the labor pains of injustice and sung through the sin of slavery. Our communities are stitched with the threads of deferred dreams and realized hopes. We are made with the fabric of struggle for a purpose-filled existence while striving to be true to ourselves, our ancestry, and our native land.

The intent of this book is fourfold:

1. To empower persons to teach and learn the scriptures;
2. To enrich persons' lives with some elements of African-American culture;
3. To equip persons with resources for making meaning[2] and sense about their experiences; and,
4. To encourage persons to become increasingly faithful disciples of Jesus Christ.

For Christian education to be effective in African-American communities, it must have cultural integrity with the African-American experiences and traditions. In this regard, cultural integrity means respect for the particular experiences and traditions of African Americans. If Christian education can demonstrate this respect, it will both enhance the cultural heritage of African Americans and deepen African-American expressions of Christian commitment and faith.

It is necessary for Christian education to uphold cultural integrity for African Americans. Christian education for the Black church involves, fundamentally, processes of teaching scripture in light of the experiences and traditions of African Americans. Christian education involves the processes of teaching the scriptures with respect for the experiences and traditions of particular cultures, so that persons may become transformed and share in God's transforming activity in history.

Focusing on this understanding of Christian education has several implications. One, *there is a shift from reaching understandings and making decisions based solely on external knowledge to an integration of knowledge and experience.* Tradition and experience are presented with the recognition that teachers teach and learners learn *and* that teachers learn and learners teach. All persons involved in the interaction become subject to God's truth made known in Jesus Christ. This understanding of Christian education is less like adding facts to make greater sums of knowledge and more like elements interacting to make something different from the originals.

Second, teaching scripture with cultural integrity *upholds respect for the traditions and experiences of African Americans while allowing for new interpretations of meaning.*

> [T]radition is also the handing down of these religious meanings so that they can be taken up anew, retold, actualized. . . . [T]radition makes adaptation possible and necessary. We receive the tradition as a responsibility to contemporize it, to engage it with the crucial issues of an ever-changing world. Therefore, we recognize this tradition itself to have occurred from the accumulated efforts of past generations to do the same thing: deal with their own times in light of treasured religious meanings handed down to them from their past.[3]

The formation of culture emerges from historical experience, yet it is open-ended. All persons are potential participants in the shaping of culture. This view of tradition recognized that African Americans' historical experiences are not closed off from today's learners.

When the goal is to teach scripture with cultural integrity, then the teacher seeks to make accessible the traditions, narratives, and experiences of African Americans. The transcendent truths from the traditions and experiences of past generations continue to be identified, possessed, and used in teaching about and living a life of faith in Jesus Christ.

A third implication is that teaching scripture with cultural integrity *makes it possible for future generations to get the story straight.* History is too often embellished to tell how persons wished experiences happened rather than the way they really happened.

> As *criticism,* history questions the adequacy of accepted stories and analyzes the "elements" used to construct them. . . . [H]istory presents a story in such a way that it becomes part of a people's public understanding and thereby provides a context and resource for public decision-making about the kind of world those people seek to construct.[4]

Time provides learners with an opportunity to reconstruct life experiences soberly.

The narratives and traditions of African Americans need to be analyzed and critiqued with a clear eye on the assumptions that guide one's evaluation. The result can be the presentation of the African American story which can empower African Americans and other persons and cultures to grow in Christian faith.

This book is organized in two parts. Part I presents four strategies for teaching scripture in African-American communities. Chapter 1 presents "The Story Strategy[5] of Education." It integrates the African-American experience of storytelling into a strategy of teaching and learning. The story strategy is primarily concerned with the questions of identity and vocation. Teachers and learners give attention to the questions "Who am I as a person of God?" and "What am I called to do?" in light of a peculiar history and a particular place and time.

Chapter 2 introduces "The Exile Strategy of Education." The strategy gives attention to the African-American experiences and traditions that emerged from the experiences of geographical and social dislocation. The exile strategy emphasizes the biblical call to God's people to live in harmony with all of creation. The strategy uses just and harmonic behavior as a process for shaping right beliefs.

Chapter 3 presents "The Sanctuary Strategy of Education." The strategy acknowledges that community is the essential character of life. It builds upon two fundamental pillars of African-American communal life: the experience of sanctuary and the tradition of worship. The goal of the strategy is to help teachers and learners identify and claim reconciliation as the way of Christians.

Chapter 4 presents "The Exodus Strategy of Education." The Exodus focuses attention on the African-American experience and tradition of social engagement toward the fulfillment of the biblical mandate of justice and equality for all people of the earth. Social analysis is a primary tool of the strategy for knowing and doing the work of Christ. The biblical themes of justice and liberation are primary, and the intended responses include that of service to one's neighbor and community.

Part II discusses some critical issues that surround the nature and tasks of Christian education as it is influenced by culture. Chapter 5, "Christian Education with Cultural Specificity," broadens the discussion beyond ethnic racial boundaries. It provides the basis for understanding how other cultural distinctions shape and give meaning to what is known and the way persons come to know. For example, regional factors—such as rural/urban, Northerner/Southerner, Easterner/Westerner, native language, and kinds of education received—influence persons' cultural heritage and their expressions of Christian commitments and faith.

Chapter 6, "Teaching Insights from African-American Churches," suggests four related issues of Christian education in African-American communities. These concerns are not unique to the African-American church. They are, however, significant as African Americans integrate and interact with the concerns from a particular historical journey.

Teaching scripture with cultural integrity provides a chance for teachers and learners to hear the Word of God in distinct and meaningful ways; gain ways and means of communicating the importance of their experiences, stories, and traditions to audiences unfamiliar with their history and experiences; and become more able than before to see and support creative and constructive responses to God's abiding presence in the world.

PART I

CHAPTER 1
THE STORY STRATEGY OF EDUCATION

In the year that King Uzziah died, I saw the Lord sitting on a throne, high and lofty; and the hem of his robe filled the temple. Seraphs were in attendance above him; each had six wings: with two they covered their faces, and with two they covered their feet, and with two they flew. And one called to another and said: "Holy, holy, holy is the Lord of hosts; the whole earth is full of his glory."

The pivots on the thresholds shook at the voices of those who called, and the house filled with smoke. And I said: "Woe is me! I am lost, for I am a man of unclean lips, and I live among a people of unclean lips; yet my eyes have seen the King, the Lord of hosts!"

Then one of the seraphs flew to me, holding a live coal that had been taken from the altar with a pair of tongs. The seraph touched my mouth with it and said: "Now that this has touched your lips, your guilt has departed and your sin is blotted out. Then I heard the voice of the Lord saying, "Whom shall I send, and who will go for us?" And I said, "Here am I; send me!" (Isaiah 6:1-8).

Teaching Scripture and the Metaphor of Story

Scripture is taught so that persons may become formed and transformed into faithful disciples of Jesus Christ. The aim is for learners to claim the life of Jesus as their own and to embrace an identity in the fullness of their lives. But the formative and transformative processes must not ignore the cultural context through which identity emerges or faith is expressed. Culture is the container of a community's experience and the agent of the community's expressions of faithfulness and faithlessness. Jesus, within the boundaries of a specific culture, fulfilled his responsibility to God. African Americans are also called to identify, claim, and embrace Christian discipleship within our specific culture.

"Story" is the metaphorical reference for this strategy. The metaphor of *story* has at least three dimensions. One, *story* refers to the history of African Americans. Two, *story* is used to refer to particular passages from scripture. For example, we speak of the story of creation, the story of the Exodus, the story of Jesus, the parables, and so forth. The third dimension of *story* emphasizes its theological aspects. It refers to the drama of God's actions in history.

Jesus of Nazareth is the story's main character, and through the writings, witness, traditions, and actions of the Christian community the drama continues to unfold. The story strategy understands these three dimensions in dynamic relationship.

Teaching scripture as story allows God's story to become a guiding light for the learner. Resources for faith are provided that can support a person's character development. Images are presented that can nurture a construction of Christian identity that is faithful to the church.

Teaching scripture as "story" and connecting scripture to African-American experiences and traditions make possible the release of God's life-changing power into the lives of persons. Hearers become inspired and encouraged to identify their story with the scripture. Readers are equipped to relate and broaden their personal experiences in light of their social existence. Learners are empowered to judge and redefine what is meaningful in their lives.

The oral tradition of storytelling in African-American communities is the cultural experience that serves as the basis for the story strategy of teaching scripture. The experience and tradition of storytelling are upheld, respected, and built upon.

Storytelling has had an important role among African Americans. In our communities the oral tradition has been the primary way in which storytelling has occurred.

> In many areas of Africa . . . there is usually a system of professional folklorists, or "rememberers," who keep track of the traditions. Past events are recounted, with contemporary happenings linked in through the art of improvisation. (For example) the Rwanda . . . support specialists who are employed as a sort of walking library transmitting their knowledge only to direct successors. Among African peoples with centralized governments, the phenomenon of the official whose duty it is to recite the history at the ruler's court is common.[6]

Storytelling has shaped the view African Americans have of social existence and personal identity. Storytelling has provided us with a basic resource for understanding our existence.

The Strategy

Storytelling in the oral tradition enables personal perception to interact with social experience. The interaction itself is something other than either the personal perception or the social experience was alone. The dynamic interaction creates a new reality.

This paradigm includes a six-step process that may be used in relation to a variety of biblical content.

1. Presentation of an African-American story
2. Identification and recall of a personal story
3. Presentation of a biblical story
4. Critical reflection
5. Restructuring the personal story
6. Commitment to incorporate and make use of the restructured story as a guide for responding to God's movement in the world

The Strategy Applied

STEP 1. PRESENTATION OF AN AFRICAN-AMERICAN STORY

"I Am Blessed but You Are Damned" is an autobiographical story of an African-American slave.[7]

One day while in the field plowing I heard a voice. I jumped because I thought it was my master coming to scold and whip me for plowing up some more corn. I looked but saw no one. Again the voice called, "Morte! Morte!" With this I stopped, dropped the plow, and started running, but the voice kept on speaking to me saying, "Fear not, my little one, for behold! I come to bring you a message of truth."

Everything got dark, and I was unable to stand any longer, I began to feel sick, and there was a great roaring. I tried to cry and move but was unable to do either. I looked up and saw that I was in a new world. There were plants and animals, and all, even the water where I stooped down to drink, began to cry out, "I am blessed but you are damned! I am blessed but you are damned!" With this I began to pray, and a voice on the inside began to cry, "Mercy! Mercy!" As I prayed an angel came and touched me, and I looked new. I looked at my hands and they were new; I looked at my feet and they were new. I looked and saw my old body suspended over a burning pit by a small web like a spider web. I again prayed, and there came a soft voice saying, "My little one, I have loved you with an everlasting love. You are this day made alive and freed from hell. You are a chosen vessel unto the Lord. Be upright before me, and I will guide you unto all truth. My grace is sufficient for you. Go, and I am with you. Preach the gospel, and I will preach with you. You are henceforth the salt of the earth."

I then began to shout and clap my hands. All the time a voice on the inside was crying, "I am so glad! I am so glad!" About this time an angel appeared before me and said with a loud voice, "Praise God! Praise God!" I looked to the east, and there was a large throne lifted high up, and thereon sat one, even God. He looked neither to the right nor to the left, I was afraid and fell on my face. When I was still a long way off I heard a voice from God saying, "My little one, be not afraid, for lo! many wondrous works will I perform through thee. Go in peace, and lo! I am with you always." All this he said but opened not his mouth while speaking. Then all those about the throne shouted and said, "Amen."

I then came to myself again and shouted and rejoiced. After so long a time I recovered my real senses and realized that I had been plowing and that the horse had run off with the plow and dragged down much of the corn. I was afraid and began to pray, for I knew the master would whip me most unmercifully when he found that I had plowed up the corn.

About this time my master came down the field. I became very bold and answered him when he called me. He asked me very roughly how I came to plow up the corn, and where the horse and plow were, and why I had got along so slowly. I told him that I had been talking with God Almighty, and that it was God who had plowed up the corn. He looked at me very strangely, and suddenly I fell for shouting, and I shouted and began to preach. The words seemed to flow from my lips. When I had finished I had a deep feeling of satisfaction and no longer dreaded the whipping I knew I would get. My master looked at me and seemed to tremble. He told me to catch the horse, stumbling down the corn rows. Here again I became weak and began to be afraid for the whipping. After I had gone some distance down the rows, I became dazed and again fell to the ground. In a vision I saw Gabriel. And a voice said to me, "Behold your sins as a great mountain. But they shall be rolled away. Go in peace, fearing no man, for lo I have cut loose your stammering tongue and unstopped your deaf ears. A witness shalt thou be, and thou shalt speak to multitudes, and they shall hear. My word has gone forth, and it is power. Be strong, and lo! I am with you even until the world shall end. Amen."

I looked, and the angel Gabriel lifted his hand, and my sins, that had stood as a mountain, began to roll away. I saw them as they rolled over into the great pit. They fell to the bottom, and there was a great noise. I saw old Satan with a host of his angels hop from the pit, and there they began to stick out their tongues at me and make motions as if to lay hands on me and drag me back into the pit. I cried out, "Save me! Save me, Lord!" And like a flash there gathered around me a host of angels, even a great number, with their backs to me and their faces to the outer world. Then stepped one in the direction of the pit. Old Satan and his angels, growling with anger and trembling with fear, hopped back into the pit. Finally again there came a voice unto me saying, "Go in peace and fear not, for lo! I will throw around you a strong arm of protection. Neither shall your oppressors be able to confound you. I will make your enemies feed you and those who despise you take you in. Rejoice and be exceedingly glad, for I have saved you through grace by faith, not of yourself but as a gift of God. Be strong and fear not. Amen."

I rose from the ground shouting and praising God. Within me there was a crying, "Holy! Holy! Holy is the Lord!"

I must have been in this trance for more than an hour. I went on to the barn and found my master there waiting for me. Again I began to tell him of my experience. I do not recall what he did to me afterwards. I felt burdened down and that preaching was my only relief. When I had finished I felt a great love in my heart that made me feel like stooping and kissing the very ground. My master sat watching and listening to me, and then he began to cry. He turned from me and said to me, in a broken voice, "Morte, I believe you are a preacher. From now on you can preach to the people here on my place in the old shed by the creek. But tomorrow morning, Sunday, I want you to preach to my family and neighbors. So put on your best clothes and be in front of the big house early in the morning, about nine o'clock."

I was so happy that I did not know what to do. I thanked my master and then God, for I felt that he was with me. Throughout the night I went from cabin to cabin, rejoicing and spreading the news.

The next morning at the time appointed I stood up on two planks in front of the porch of the big house and, without a Bible or anything, I began to preach to my master and the people. My thoughts came so fast that I could hardly speak fast enough. My soul caught on fire, and soon I had them all in tears. I told them that God had a chosen people and that he had raised me up as an example of his matchless love. I told them that they must be born again and that their souls must be freed from the shackles of hell.

Ever since that day I have been preaching the gospel and am not a bit tired. I can tell anyone about God in the darkest hour of midnight, for it is written on my heart. Amen.

Stories about ancient African experiences and the heritage of Africans in America serve as sources of inspiration for many African Americans. Recalling the journey from slavery to freedom in America often equips us with courage. The African and African-American traditions of storytelling have been the primary instruments to transmit these experiences and stories. As we African Americans hear stories of our heritage, many of us experience a sense of bonding with past generations. Through the spoken word, African Americans find encouragement and validation of ancestral traditions and experiences. Also, we experience social cohesion and communal bonding in the present.

The first step of the story strategy serves to focus and prepare the attention of the teacher and learner. It is assumed that learners have the ability and interest to attend to stories and experiences embedded in the heritage of their culture.

The very nature of storytelling leads to the suspicion that everything and anything is to be included. This is not so. The selection and telling of the African-American and biblical stories set the boundaries for concerns to be discussed and investigated.

Telling stories from one's cultural legacy allows for entrée into the world and lives of learners. The way one looks at an issue or concern affects the way he or she understands the issue or concern. The learner's view is critical. This does not mean that the cultural story can simply govern the biblical story, but teaching scripture necessarily involves attempting to reach the hearts and minds of learners at their deepest level of existence. Persons seldom allow strangers or even loved ones into the closets of their hearts and minds.

The learner needs ways and means of breaking through the clutter of daily activity and surface conversation. By telling stories of one's cultural heritage, a teacher has the potential to crack open the doors and make contact with significant aspects of the learner's existence.

The following questions can help persons define the boundaries for their learning. These questions may be used with other cultural stories, too. *What issues do you understand the character(s) in the story to be concerned with?* (For example, concerns of identity and life-task.) *What is your experience with these or similar issues? How do you explain and make sense of this story? In what way(s) does the experience correspond to your life?*

Some learners may not identify with the story. Some persons may answer that they have changed jobs or professions for work that is meaningful. Or, learners who work as custodians or groundskeepers may speak of their work in terms of God's movement in their lives. They may see how caring for property and land is related to serving God and neighbor.

What are some ways in which you may set out to address concerns raised in the story? Learners may begin by closely examining their daily work in relation to God's activity in their lives. They may talk about their inner thoughts and feelings with family and friends. Teachers may ask family and friends to talk about the constructive values and behaviors learners uphold.

STEP 2. IDENTIFICATION AND COMMUNICATION OF A PERSONAL STORY

The life of the learner is an important element in the story strategy. The learner, as the "living human document,"[8] has the opportunity, potential, and responsibility for responding to the presented African-American story. Because the personal stories of the learners are a part of the content, the teaching/learning experience is never totally predetermined. Learners must build the bridge that connects their personal stories with social experiences of the African-American heritage.

Personal stories may be constructed by using several kinds of categories. For example, persons may identify and construct their story with specific attention given to persons, settings, and circumstances. Learners may give attention to emotions and feelings, such as fear or love, or to sensations, such as comfort or pain. They may concentrate on individual behaviors, relationships, or group interactions. Their stories may be centered around causes and consequences or a combination of elements.

After learners have identified and organized a personal story, they may wish for the group to engage in conversation. Persons may discuss their personal story from various stances, such as its opportunities and limitations in light of the African-American story told.

What are your major concerns? Learners may voice frustration about not understanding their life as a story. They may talk about the fear of not having a story or about their story not making sense or having meaning.

How do you perceive and describe your current place in the world? The learners' workplaces may be places of enormous affirmation or hostility. They may view themselves at the beginning of a long and hopeful journey. Some may be barely holding on to their jobs or unemployed. All of these experiences are occasions for persons to understand the distinction between vocation (our lived relationship with God) and occupation.

What are your current limitations? privileges? responsibilities?

Learners may discuss some missed opportunities in response to God's activity in their lives. Some may be joyful about present chances to do God's will. Some may express frustration about the difficulties that come with living in faithful relationship with God in the workplace, at home, or in other settings.

What are your points of satisfaction? Learners who are students, secretaries, managers, or who work inside the home may express joy about how their work supports the efforts of others in pursuit of common goals. Teachers, administrators, and health, social, and government workers may share the happiness that comes with serving others. Laborers, salespersons, and business executives may talk about the satisfaction that comes with having products and services that meet the needs and desires of clients.

STEP 3. PRESENTATION OF THE BIBLICAL STORY

The primary purpose of the story strategy is to teach the scripture. Presentation of the biblical story offers a reference for learners as they construct meaning. The scripture story also expresses the intent of God's actions as understood by the author.

The scripture passage may be placed in the historical, cultural context of its day, but it is to be presented as a story. The intent of the writer is to be included. This will provide teachers and learners with some boundaries for interpretation of meaning. The use of imagination is to be encouraged. When parallel situations come to mind, their expression may be encouraged. The following example presents these concerns in story form.

King Uzziah, ruler of Judah from 783 to 742 B.C., had a long and prosperous reign. "He did what was right in the sight of the Lord" (2 Kings 15:3). But King Uzziah died the year Isaiah received a call from God (Isaiah 6:1-8).

Isaiah of Jerusalem was a prophet of Judah during their most critical time in history. His résumé places him in association with leading politicians of his time. His career brought him into contact with power politics and powerful politicians. But the God of Israel called Isaiah to move beyond contemporary party politics to include heaven's view of human interests.

Isaiah argued that political problems could not be resolved without the perspective of God's will for humanity. He witnessed first-hand Samaria's exile and the break-up of Judah. Still, he remained full of hope in spite of the wars and warriors that surrounded his life and the life of his people, Israel.

The primary purpose of the story strategy (and the other strategies as well) is to teach scripture. The Word of God has life-changing power, and life at this time in history is in need of sacramental change.

Scripture contains an account of God's intentions for creation, what has gone wrong, God's response to what has gone wrong, and God's hope for what creation can become. God's activity recorded in scripture makes possible our discovery of God's activity in the world today.

The scripture provides teachers and learners with a particular frame of reference. It gives shape and form to a person's view of existence. The scripture may be heard and understood in new ways as cultural and personal stories are given focused attention, and the cultural and personal stories may be illumined and/or revised by scripture. The scripture constructs and orders one's life view in light of particular experiences and traditions of a culture.

Scripture as a frame of reference is authoritative. It serves as the referent to which all concerns are related and by which all issues are judged. For the church, scripture is the plumb line of life. The church understands itself, its reason for being, and its destiny in terms of scripture. The church is the people of the Word.

Step 3 may begin with the telling of the scripture story. A discussion would follow. The intent in this step is to invite learners to place the African-American story, their personal story, and the scripture narrative in relation to one another. Questions that may help the learner reach the objective include the following: *Who are the persons with whom you relate? What are the similarities and differences between your life experiences and those of the characters in the scripture? What are the similarities and differences among your personal history, the cultural story, and the scripture?* For example, learners may quickly note that Isaiah's call was to speak on behalf of God. Persons may not understand themselves as prophets or preachers. However, they may see how care for family members or for persons with whom they work is a response to God's call and how that response is of equal value to God.

What insight do you gain from the biblical story for your situation? What importance, if any, does the passage have for you? Responses may include learners' identification with a personal or group experience through which they clearly see God's movement and feel compelled to answer. Some may question or have no idea about God's action in their life. Some may doubt God's presence in light of present pain and misery. If so, the passage may become for them a word of hope and promise.

STEP 4. CRITICAL REFLECTION

The stories persons live by are not value-free; nor are the values persons embrace always the values of God. In one respect, human stories are the carriers of the ideas, experiences, and possessions persons hold important. When we state that scripture presents a description of what has gone wrong, we assume a particular understanding of what is of importance even when it is not mentioned.

The stories by which persons live support their perspectives and behaviors. Yet, if change and growth are to occur, these stories need to be examined in light of scripture.

> [I]t is painful and threatening to give up a familiar myth, even when it is limiting your opportunities. Established myths are sometimes so central to your identity that to denounce them, though they are dysfunctional, means suffering . . . 'little deaths.' . . . [I]n the ancient mystery schools, one is required to die to one story in order to be reborn to a larger one. The soul's development is said to begin 'with the wounding of the psyche by the Larger Story. . . . The old and the emerging typically engage in a struggle deep within you, a contest between the dying and the unborn, for the dominance of your perceptions, values, and motivations. . . .
>
> A personal myth is a constellation of beliefs, feelings, and images that is organized around a core theme and addresses one of four domains: . . . (1) explain the world—the urge to comprehend the natural world in a meaningful way; (2) guide personal development—the search for a marked pathway through the succeeding epochs of human life; (3) provide social direction—the need to establish secure and fulfilling relationships within a community; and (4) address spiritual longings—the longing to know one's part in the vast wonder and mystery of the cosmos.[9]

Human development evolves through processes of crisis and transition. Using personal, cultural, and biblical stories that present and illuminate the concerns of identity and/or vocation, work together toward personal growth and development.

The stage of critical reflection assumes that persons have not yet embodied the fullness of Jesus Christ. There is work to be done. The will and actions of humanity are not completely aligned with the will and activity of God.

Four questions may help you begin the process of critical reflection: With what elements of the stories do you identify strongly? What aspects of your story become threatened as you give attention to the three stories? What ideas, understandings, and assumptions from your story are called into question by the African-American and biblical stories? What aspects of the cultural and biblical stories provide assurance and hope for you?

STEP 5. RESTRUCTURING THE PERSONAL STORY

Hearing the African-American and scripture stories can help persons experience transformation. These stories inspire persons to assess and reorder their lives after God's intent for them. Restructuring one's personal story permits the individual to select, pattern, and integrate new insights and behaviors into his or her life.

Three assumptions undergird this task. First, the story strategy presumes that the biblical narrative is of more value than other information when determining one's true identity and call of life. The scripture, in processes of interpretation and synthesis, functions as the balance in the scale or the magnetic north of the compass. Human knowledge is limited. Persons are not able to consider fully the transcendent nature of God's presence and power. Yet, the Christian community believes that the Word of God makes known to us the unknowable God as we seek meaning and value. The scripture provides balance for the weight of personal and social experience. The scripture brings into focus for persons (and sometimes realigns the importance of) their historical and cultural experiences and traditions.

Second, even though scripture is the balance for understanding God's authentic activity, the voice and movement of God are not limited to the pages of scripture. The stories of African Americans and the personal experiences of the learner, as well as the scripture, mutually interact to create new perspectives. All elements of the teaching/learning activity potentially have equal influence on the learner.

Finally, the restructuring of one's personal story does not assume a predetermined outcome. The story of God's power and presence in the world continues to unfold. And persons do have freedom to respond. The drama of God's unending love continues in mutual coexistence with the response of persons. The interaction of the African-American story, the personal story, and the biblical story does not predict particular thoughts, feelings, actions, or behaviors. The interaction of the stories allows the learner to receive and perceive freely. And learners are free to respond in meaningful ways depending on their particular circumstances.

Several questions may assist teachers in Step 5. *What understandings or images do you now have about God's intentions for your life?* Some students may want to read and study the scriptures more regularly. Others may respond by describing the specific relationships that they are called to enhance and support. Still others may connect God's call to their daily work.

What conditions need to exist in order for you to accept the challenge to begin using the reconstructed story as a guide for living in response to God? Responses may include support from family and friends, an exploration of new job opportunities, a close look at present obligations, skills, and experiences.

In what way(s) do these stories make you aware of other movements of God in your life? Some learners may begin to understand God's activity in their life as an inner voice of consciousness. Some may reflect on how God spoke to them through past conversations with friends. Still others may look to God's created order and become aware of God's presence and power among them, moving them to say, "Lord, here I am. Send me!"

STEP 6. COMMITMENT TO INCORPORATE AND MAKE USE OF THE RESTRUCTURED OR NEW STORY

Teaching scripture is not done for the purpose of preparing biblical scholars. Little value is seen in acquiring biblical knowledge for the sake of knowing a mass of information. The purpose of teaching scripture is so that persons may make their response to God in and through communities of Christians. Teaching scripture occurs so that persons may take up their ministry and continue to respond to the call of God.

Step 6 may begin with an exploration of several questions: *What is one attitude, quality, or behavior you can embrace that will illuminate your understanding of your reconstructed story?* Patience or stillness may be one behavior. Patience and stillness are not passive but active behaviors. They require of learners the effort to stand still and behold God's salvation. Patience and stillness may move learners toward becoming God's heart, hands, and feet for the world.

Integrity is another quality that may help learners live out their new or reconstructed story. Integrity will allow learners to uphold past work and the vocational opportunities that remain to be done. Integrity will help persons accept themselves as becoming responsive to God's activity and will.

In what way(s) are you moved to relate differently with others? What feelings do you have as you explore working with other persons and groups in response to your story? The story strategy of education is communal at the foundational level and at the level of individual responses. Persons are related to the stories and actions of the African-American heritage and the Bible. And the future direction of the stories is bonded as well. The interrelatedness of the learners' existence is to be highlighted as the development and reconstruction of stories occur. The common ground upon which individual stories are built and the common future to which the stories point may inspire and motivate persons toward reflecting upon their life in light of the African-American and biblical hopes and dreams.

Conclusion

The story strategy is designed to teach scripture to African-American Christians in ways that affirm our culture and influence our understanding of ourselves and our place in God's world. This strategy attempts to address the question, "What are the stories, symbols, and traditions of African-Americans and Christianity that make meaningful participation in the Christian tradition possible?" The story strategy hopes to inspire learners to continue those traditions, and it seeks to identify and revise inadequacies of an individual's personal story in order to live in harmony with God's revelation in scripture.

The story strategy is deeply concerned with the personal and the corporate dimensions of Christian faith and practice. By combining personal, cultural, and biblical stories, the story strategy seeks to integrate and deepen these dimensions in the personal, social, political, economic, and religious life of a community.

The story strategy of education provides us as African-American Christians the cultural context in which to explore and reflect critically on the various aspects of our lives. Persons have a chance to become acquainted with stories from the African-American heritage and to discover meanings of the scripture through a culturally sensitive lens. The strategy allows persons to raise questions about who God intends for them to become. And it challenges learners to take possession of and use their reconstructed narratives as a guide in responding to God's ongoing activity in the world.

CHAPTER 2
THE EXILE STRATEGY OF EDUCATION

By the rivers of Babylon—there we sat down and there we wept
when we remembered Zion.
On the willows there we hung up our harps.
For there our captors asked us for songs,
and our tormentors asked for mirth, saying,
"Sing us one of the songs of Zion!"

How could we sing the Lord's song in a foreign land?
If I forget you, O Jerusalem, let my right hand wither!
Let my tongue cling to the roof of my mouth,
if I do not remember you,
if I do not set Jerusalem above my highest joy! (Psalm 137:1-6).

Teaching Scripture and the Theme of Exile

The scripture is taught so that persons may make the Word of God part of their lives. The primary intent is to prepare and empower persons to become faithful to God and to live a life of faith, hope, and love. The scripture is taught in order to challenge persons to uphold Christian faith and love in daily actions.

An exile strategy of education is developed to encourage persons to employ the scripture in their conduct and relations. Meaning can emerge through the ordering of one's actions and behavior—what persons do and what persons desire to become.

If persons are to live and act with integrity, their present situation cannot be separated from its past. Human existence is characterized by its freedom within limits. Part of the limitation of human life is its ties with its social, historical, and cultural roots. The heritage of African Americans holds part of their promise. A growing awareness of their heritage may encourage African-American Christians to live and act with integrity according to the scripture. Respect for their culture empowers African Americans to embrace the scripture in their day-to-day conduct.

The theme of "exile" is used as an interpretive "lens" to focus this educational strategy. Teaching scripture through the lens of exile makes it possible to address the human longing for harmony. The lens of exile allows persons to see the whole scripture in terms of assembly and dispersion, relatedness and estrangement, enjoyment and brokenness. The understanding of enjoyment and brokenness includes the experience of intensity of feelings, but it is not limited to emotions. Enjoyment and brokenness also refer to the acts of persons in their becoming and evolution—including acts of joining affectively in harmonious relationships. The Bible narrates experiences and images of God and the people of God that give focus to the metaphor of exile and the longing to live in harmony.

When the Israelites lived in Mesopotamia and Babylon, they were living in exile and awaiting their return home. As exiles living in dispersion, they longed for reunification and assembly. The Law of Moses, which was given to the Jews in the wilderness, and the Sermon on the Mount both dealt with the ordering of relationships among people. The Israelites experienced themselves as exiles in brokenness (caused by self-centeredness and pride), and they hoped for ordered and right relations. When Joshua presented his testimony at Shechem (Joshua 24) (like Jesus journeying to Jerusalem), he was seeking to extend the will of God. These narratives tell of the challenge of every generation to participate in the processes that extend God's will and promise. They present a longing to live in harmony with God and a "response–ability" to order one's actions accordingly.

The theme of exile as a focusing lens for teaching scripture allows us as African-American Christians to be faithful to our history and experience. The exile serves as a reference in making sense out of the dispersion of our ancestors from Africa. The exile provides a perspective so that persons may embrace a history that includes being stolen, sold into captivity, and transported to and transplanted in an alien land.

Exile speaks to the African-American experience in America. That experience has been an experiment of social arrangements. At times African Americans have been relegated to slavery. At times we have lived as second-class citizens. Even our ghettos have been drastically different from the ghettos of other Americans.

Exile evokes the African-American adventure toward enjoyment and sustains the struggle to realize our true and full character as a people. It ushers in understanding of the way ancestors upheld ties with kin in opposition to the slave master's auction block. It accounts for the way African Americans have worked to keep alive some rites and rituals in the face of an ideology of "the melting pot." ("The melting pot" has been an American experiment which has led to the dismantling of cultures across racial, ethnic, and regional boundaries—not only for African Americans but for all.)

The biblical image of exile challenges us as African Americans to remember the stories of our ancestors as they resisted enemies who once forbade the use of their native tongue. An understanding of exile can inspire African Americans to swim against future tides that threaten their heritage. Teaching the scripture through the lens of exile empowers African Americans to act as a subject, rather than just being acted on; to uphold their heritage and enrich their present existence; and to make possible the enjoyment of their future as a people of God. Home for the Israelites was a return to the Land of Promise, a specific geographical site—real dirt and rubble. Home for African Americans is a return to the cultural experiences that give shape and vitality to their existence as a people.

The Strategy

An exile strategy of education empowers persons so that they may move toward harmony with all of God's creation. This is accomplished by engaging the scripture in practical conduct. The educational method is social interaction and participation.

> Faith is communicated by a community of believers and the meaning of faith is developed by its members out of their history, by their interaction with each other, and in relation to the events that take place in their lives. . . . The congregation, then, is a school of faith. All that the congregation does is both a means of communicating the faith and a subject of investigation.[10]

The methodology assumes that persons have the capacity to nurture one another toward responsible conduct. Through the nurturing process of social interaction, persons can grow to increase their realization of their moral and ethical behavior. They can discover that their truth claims about the living Christ are embedded in the everyday order, action, conduct, and relations of Christians. The exile strategy of education attempts to build upon this understanding.

The process of an exile strategy of education is fourfold. The four steps include:

1. *Acknowledging the Condition*—Presents information from the African-American experience. The intent is to make persons aware of the harmony or disharmony, wholeness or brokenness that exists.

2. *Fashioning the Heart*—Provides the opportunity for persons to initiate conduct that leads toward harmony with God and all of creation. This segment is grounded in the belief that persons may come to know God, become encouraged to live on behalf of God, and be equipped to fill their lives with meaning by the practices of faithful living.

3. *Previewing and Expanding the Horizon*—Places before the learner the scripture so that it may be in dialogue with the African-American experience or tradition. The expectation is that the scripture will support and/or challenge the learner's moral and ethical conduct and actions.

4. *Reflecting*—Allows learners to think about their conduct in relation to all of life. This segment adds the processes of the intellect to the task of making meaning.

Following is an example of how the four segments of an education strategy of exile may be applied.

An Application of the Exile Strategy

STEP 1. ACKNOWLEDGING THE CONDITION

The poem "I, Too" by Langston Hughes is an example of a cultural text that expresses the African-American experience and the hope to move toward harmony.

I, Too

I, too, sing America.
I am the darker brother.
They send me to eat in the kitchen
when company comes,
But I laugh,
and eat well,
And grow strong.

Tomorrow,
I'll be at the table

When the company comes.
Nobody'll dare
Say to me,
"Eat in the kitchen,"
Then.

Besides,
They'll see how beautiful I am
and be ashamed—
I, too, am American.[11]

Many African Americans believe that living in harmony with the created order and with the Creator is the goal of life. Harmony as the goal of life for African Americans has both a transcendent, other-world dimension, and an immanent, this-world dimension. African Americans, with a view toward the world beyond, uphold the goal of harmony by living according to laws and principles that govern the universe. With a view toward this world, we affirm the goal of harmony primarily in terms of social arrangements.

The African-American orientation toward harmony with God and creation emerges from the African-American experiences on the soil of both lands. From the soil of Africa this understanding emerges out of the African sense of the religious. African religion can be defined as those patterns of belief and behavior that give definition to African ways of being in the world. This includes the manner in which Africans act, judge, decide, identify, and address life's critical concerns. Therefore, an African's view of harmony is revealed by her or his sense of community. For tribal religions this takes a particular form.

> The tribe is nothing if it is not a religious unit, just as much as it is domestic, economic and political. From this derives the power of its morality. . . . The tribe is, in a sense, then a church; it is a community bound together in common allegiance to a common ancestor in whom its members believe. It would scarcely be worthy of its continued existence, indeed it would probably cease to exist, if it did not uphold its beliefs. But belief, for the African tribe, does not merely emerge in times of crisis; it permeates and motivates everyday life.[12]

The tribal connection of the religious with the domestic, economic, and political is evidence of African harmony. Connecting common beliefs with those of the ancestors binds the tribe to that which transcends everyday life.

In the United States, African Americans' experiences of life as a tireless struggle for justice and equality is the root of their hope for harmony. In his sermon, "Our God Is Able," Martin Luther King, Jr., expressed the struggle most vividly.

> These changes are not mere political and sociological shifts. They represent the passing of systems that were born in injustice, nurtured in inequality, and reared in exploitation. They represent the inevitable decay of any system based on principles that are not in harmony with the moral laws of the universe. When in future generations [persons] look back upon these turbulent, tension-packed days through which we are passing, they will see God working through history for the salvation of [humanity]. . . . In our sometimes difficult and often lonesome walk up freedom's road, we do not walk alone. God walks with us. [God] has placed within the very structure of this universe certain absolute moral laws. We can neither defy nor break them. If we disobey them, they will break us. The forces of evil may temporarily conquer truth, but truth will ultimately conquer its conqueror.[13]

The ability of African Americans to describe and face the actual condition of brokenness is at least partly a consequence of belief in the stronger power and eternal order of a loving and just God. The exile strategy of education offers ways and methods for African Americans to engage in and to reflect on fellowship with God. Exploration of African-Americans' contemporary experiences also may lead teachers and learners to discover significant dimensions of those experiences. Contemporary experiences of assembly and dispersion may focus the action and discussion on entry into new communities, homelessness, relocation, or transitions from old into new school or work environments.

In "Mother to Son" the African-American poet Langston Hughes wrote about ways in which social disenfranchisement resulted in less than quality living. Experiences of inequality have shaped African-Americans' hope for harmony in the social arrangements of this world. While we as African Americans have in general lacked access to political power, we have sought help from a higher plane. In spite of our experience of injustice and oppression, we believe in the existence of an eternal and universal order, and have dared to live accordingly.

Contemporary experiences may concern behavior and thinking about the way persons live as subjects, rather than as objects, in the world. Actions and reflections may lead persons to identify issues about which they have intense feeling, such as the quality or lack of quality in public education, the deterioration of the inner cities, employment, unemployment, under-employment, war, drug use and abuse, human sexuality, or care of the environment.

STEP 2. FASHIONING THE HEART

In this step African-American learners are invited and encouraged to identify, possess, and practice biblical habits that may lead toward living in harmony with God and all of creation. This step does not presuppose that the scripture gives the right or ethical response to every specific situation. Rather it upholds the view that faith involves more than verbal accent to propositions of truth.

For this step in the exile strategy, the faithful engagement of scripture does not suggest mimicking biblical behavior. Duplicating the conduct of biblical characters or of contemporary Christians can be a less than authentic response to the Word of God. The integrity of persons can only be preserved where the freedom to respond prevails.

Two guidelines that clarify the meaning of an authentic response to scripture for the purpose of fashioning the heart come from the work of Immanuel Kant. In his views on morality, Kant defined two key principles: the categorical imperative and the practical imperative.

The categorical imperative invites persons to "act as if the maxim of thy act were to become by the will a universal law of nature." This principle agrees in many ways with the Judeo-Christian heritage and has an affinity in American culture. In biblical literature the Mosaic Law commands, "Whatever is hurtful to you, do ye even so to them." The Sermon on the Mount contains the opposite command: "All things whatsoever ye would that men should do to you, do ye even so to them" (Matthew 7:12, KJV). Persons are encouraged to conduct themselves in a manner in which they could will that everyone (universally and categorically) follow their act.

Kant's practical imperative on the other hand stated, "Treat every man as an end in himself, and never as a means only." Used as a guideline, this can serve to prevent persons from using others as instruments or objects toward other ends.

These principles may help persons use their individual freedom responsibly when engaging the scripture in contemporary settings. The principles function as points of reference while allowing persons to respond with integrity. Together the principles can keep persons from using a double standard and/or from becoming too narrow in the search of scripture for life habits that fashion the heart. Kant's principles remind us of the need to distinguish between what applies to all persons and what is individual, without using a double standard.

Beyond the concern to avoid duplicity, Step 2 acknowledges that harmonious living embraces belief, and yet is more than belief. Belief may be distinguished from faith as presented in Wilfred C. Smith's *Faith and Belief.* On one hand, belief involves the formulation of ideas and is primarily assigned to the work of the intellect. Smith wrote:

> [B]elieving has come to be the straightforward and almost innocent interpretation of what religious people do in the modern world when they take a given position. For they are seen, rather naturally, as taking it as some sort of ideational venture; and, as one possible venture among others. . . . [14]

Belief focuses on conceptualizing and thinking about a subject. It is possible for a person to believe, yet not to live faithfully.

On the other hand, faith implies involvement in the world on behalf of God. Smith wrote:

> Faith is deeper, richer, more personal. It is engendered and sustained by a religious tradition, in some cases and to some degree by its doctrines; but it is a quality of the person, not of the system. It is an orientation of the personality, to oneself, to one's neighbor, to the universe; a total response; a way of seeing whatever one sees and of handling whatever one handles; a capacity to live at a more than mundane level; to see, to feel, to act in terms of a transcendent dimension.[15]

The purpose of Step 2 is to help learners discover, name, and describe their present habits and habits that may fashion their hearts after Christ. When learners begin to embrace the scripture in daily conduct and action, these habits begin to fashion their heart. Human action not only speaks louder than the words of mortals; human conduct gives shape to the character of the actor as well. The conduct of one's character fashions the habits of the heart while the habits of the heart inform the content of the conscience.

Scripture passages that present the meaning and experiences of discipleship may be used effectively. Examples of such passages from the Old Testament include God's call of Abraham and Abraham's response (Genesis 12); the Ten Commandments (Exodus 20:1-21); examples of responsible action (the Books of Ruth, Ezra, Nehemiah, and Esther); and responding ethically to God's initiative (Micah 6:6-8).

New Testament passages that may be used with Step 2 can include texts that explain how a loving God requires love of neighbor with deeds of service (Matthew 5-7); Christ's mission and the mission of the disciples that is directed to others (Luke 4:16-21); and examples of Christian discipline (Paul's letters).

Three kinds of response may be considered for fashioning the heart. First, persons may be invited to act and behave in ways that assume or require little risk. For example, a family may be asked to place a candle or light in a window to show support for an important issue. Second, persons may be encouraged to express conduct that requires some risk. For example, persons may be asked to declare publicly their views on an issue. Or persons may be invited to abstain from a specific act or behavior as a faithful witness. Finally, persons may respond in ways that illustrate absolute commitment. This may be expressed through persons upholding the vows taken in marriage. Or it may be demonstrated by a lifelong witness of loving everyone unconditionally. These responses move from an emphasis on the practical imperative (the personal and individual requirement) to an emphasis on the categorical imperative (the kind of habit that calls for the obedience of all).

STEP 3. PREVIEWING THE HORIZON

Teaching scripture is the fundamental task of Christian education for African-American congregations. Christian faith can be shaped by the habits of a person's behavior. But neither meaning nor understanding develops without placing habits and behavior in some frame of reference. For the Christian community the scripture places the habits of the heart in a particular context and perspective. Following is an example for achieving this aim.

The Israelite exile into Babylon is an example of the way scripture may be placed in conversation with the experience of African-

Americans. Read Psalm 137, which is an example of a biblical passage that was written in reference to the Israelite exile. With the aid of one or more Bible study helps (for example, a Bible dictionary, biblical commentaries, or a Bible atlas), one may increase her or his understanding of exile as a useful lens for faithful living.

During Babylonian exile the rulers of Babylon forced the people of Judah and Jerusalem from their homeland and took them to live in the land of Babylon. The term *exile* is here used with reference to Israel's dispersion from the nation's homeland to a foreign country.

The Babylonian exile was an important period for the people of Judah. The exile provided Judeans an occasion to discern and to reinterpret God's intent and activity amid chaos, hostility, calamity, and defeat. Many of Israel's people understood this experience as a time of God's judgment.

The exile was also a time of opportunity. If Judah accepted God's judgment that their desires and activity were not in harmony with the will and activity of God, then the God of Israel would renew their broken relationships, restore the covenant, and return them to their land. This time gave Judah the chance to restore its relationship with God and accept its role as servant on behalf of God.

The "horizon" for Christians is that which God makes possible. Step 3 gives teachers and learners a particular view of reality and specific behaviors to do. The interpretation of the biblical theme of exile provides the context for reflecting on both the conditions and habits to be practiced.

STEP 4. REFLECTING

The purpose of reflection is to help learners turn their thoughts to the interface of life-condition, habits of heart, and biblical context. Reflection has several benefits. Persons are permitted to think about and to discuss the value of their behavior, including the habits they have examined in Step 2. Persons are encouraged to inquire about the possibilities and the inadequacies of their response. In addition, learners and teachers may share insights and perspectives, exploring the connections among practices of the heart, scripture, and the African-American heritage. Finally, engaging in reflection supports the belief that reflection must occur if persons are to use their freedom responsibly.

Persons are never beyond the need for understanding. This step in the education strategy of exile allows for cleaning the lens through which persons see their conduct. Understanding makes the construction of meaning possible. And it adds to a person's ability to organize and arrange information in new and different ways. In a world that is more characterized by change than sameness, there exists a continuing need to incorporate and integrate one's experience. The exile strategy can meet this need.

Faithful living fashions a person's understanding, and understanding fuels one's faith. Understanding may support a person when the flame of inspiration grows faint. If persons are to continue their journey toward harmony with God and God's creation, the actions of faithful Christians must be informed by clear and reasoned thought.

Conclusion

Both experiences of and concerns about harmony and disharmony provide information that may serve as tests for an exile strategy of education. These experiences and concerns may represent material about assembly and dispersion, social relations and the universal order, or enjoyment and actualization of a person's human potential. A theme that permeates these three levels of harmony is the nature of human redemption. Because the exile strategy is especially concerned with learning through conduct, it is very important that all of the areas cited above are included in the learning process.

Redemption concerns the power of Christ to restore persons from conditions of brokenness to wholeness. It is about Christ's work to return persons from places of exile that they may begin anew their journey home. It is about Christ's capacity to empower persons in ways that they may act, enjoy, and participate in the processes that move toward harmony with God.

Redemption also involves human concerns that relate to persons' historical, social, and cultural experience. Redemption without change of one's perception of reality and involvement in life lacks vitality. It lacks value and importance. It is redemption without meaning.

African-American Christians are concerned about how they may act in preparation for meeting the Christ who redeems. African-American Christians are also concerned about how they are to act once they have met the Christ. Both of these concerns are about the nature of redemption. An engagement of African-Americans with their heritage, their contemporary experience, and the scripture may provide an occasion for concerns about redemption to be addressed.

This strategy's aim is to empower persons to move toward harmony with all of God's creation by engaging the scripture in practical conduct. Africans did not distinguish between what they believed and how they acted. Paden and Soja wrote, "What people do is motivated by what they believe, and what they believe springs from what they do and experience."[16] Teachers and learners come to understand God's will and humanity's fundamental relatedness with all of creation through the avenue of daily conduct. Persons can come to faithful living by living faithfully. Christian education must provide ways for learners to accept and understand God's will by experiences of responsible witness. Teaching the scripture in this way inspires persons to go beyond reducing faith to propositions of belief. Teaching the scripture through practicing faith may challenge the church to change some beliefs in light of its faithful practice.

By giving attention to experiences of social relations and behavior, persons encourage conduct and reflection on issues such as peer relations, family relations, and relations to one's community. Personal responses to the environment may also be encouraged.

CHAPTER 3
THE SANCTUARY STRATEGY OF EDUCATION

From now on, therefore, we regard no one from a human point of view; even though we once knew Christ from a human point of view, we know him no longer in that way. So if anyone is in Christ, there is a new creation: everything old has passed away; see, everything has become new! All this is from God, who reconciled us to himself through Christ, and has given us the ministry of reconciliation; that is, in Christ God was reconciling the world to himself, not counting their trespasses against them, and entrusting the message of reconciliation to us. So we are ambassadors for Christ, since God is making his appeal through us; we entreat you on behalf of Christ, be reconciled to God (2 Corinthians 5:16-20).

Teaching Scripture for Sanctuary

The term *sanctuary* in the Old Testament refers to the place(s) where God dwells. Jacob journeyed from Beersheba to Haran. One night as Jacob slept, he dreamed about angels ascending and descending. When he awoke he said, "Surely the Lord is in this place. . . . How awesome is this place! This is none other than the house of God" (Genesis 28:16, 17). Jacob named that place Bethel, and it became the northern sanctuary during the reign of Jeroboam. Moses discovered God's presence in the bush that burned, but was not consumed, and claimed that place as holy ground. In the wilderness the Israelites believed the tent was the place where God dwelt. During the reign of Solomon, after the building of the temple, the Israelites believed God resided in the holy of holies, the *qodesh haqqodashim.* After the destruction of the temple, when Israel was driven into Babylonian exile, the city of Jerusalem replaced the temple as the setting for the presence of God. Sanctuary, for the people of Israel, is a sacred place, the place where God abides.

In the New Testament the living God dwells within the *laos,* the people of God. God's presence is no longer confined to a particular place or time. The author of the Gospel of Matthew wrote that where two or three believers are gathered together in agreement, God is in their midst. Disciples of Christ are now the temple of God.

27

The Holy Spirit rests in the bodies of the believers. Wherever Christ's followers appear, God is there among them.

The sanctuary strategy of education is grounded in the understanding that God is ever-present and that God's omnipresence makes possible the transformation of every ordinary place into a sacred place. When persons recognize and respond obediently to God's presence, transformation from the ordinary to the sacred takes place and sanctuary is experienced. The sanctuary strategy of education nurtures learners toward the discovery of and faithful response to the ever-present God.

When the Word of God is taught, the power and presence of God emerge from the obscure. Learners discover God's presence amid the activity of God's creation. They are inspired to orient their lives after the example of Jesus Christ and are incorporated into the fellowship of believers. They recognize themselves by their relationship with God. They are inspired with courage to make known God's abiding presence in and through their daily actions. Sanctuary is realized.

The Strategy

Teaching scripture so that persons may discover God's presence among them is the purpose of the sanctuary strategy. Valuing African-American experiences and tradition helps learners claim their heritage and perceive the presence of God. Culturally specific texts allow learners to examine concerns that have a connection to their historical, social, and cultural environment. The strategy equips learners to readily recall images, information, and experiences from both individual and collective memories and to construct and re-construct the material retrieved in new and meaningful ways.

Teaching scripture for sanctuary unites the cries of the people with the initiating and responsive acts of God. The language, narratives, and traditions of the Christian faith empower persons to respond to the cries of life. They equip the Christian community with eyes to see and a heart to understand God's reality. When the scripture is explored and proclaimed, God's abiding presence is made known. Teaching scripture for sanctuary provides meaning and purpose for life in spite of experiences of meaninglessness. To all who seek God's saving grace, it offers hope in the God who made the heavens.

African Americans of the Christian tradition reclaim the Hebrew meaning of sanctuary as a sacred place, while upholding its Christian meaning as well. Their understanding of sanctuary comes from the life, death, and resurrection of Christ. Yet their views of sanctuary are expressed through the flesh and blood of their own culture.

In African-American culture the sanctuary has been a special place. Sanctuary has been the physical place where individual and collective self-identity has been formed, informed, and transformed. The sanctuary has been a special place where people find assurance that they have not been abandoned. They have been equipped with courage to hold on and inspired to see things not only as they existed but also as they could be. This trust was translated often into song.

In *The Soul of the Black Preacher,* Joseph A. Johnson wrote:

> The question must be asked. What were the causes which moved the black slave beyond his primitive mystic to the creation of a new type and kind of musical expression? Why did he not continue the beating out of the complex rhythm on tom-toms and drums while he uttered his cries of desperation and hopelessness? I believe that at the precise time, the psychological time, there was fused into the vestiges of the slaves' African music the spirit of Christian faith. They had been introduced to the Christian faith though in a perverted form by their masters. And this Christian faith though imperfectly presented was discovered to be, by the slaves, the precise religion for the conditions in which they found themselves. Far from their native land, customs, and traditions; despised, brutalized, degraded, and slaughtered by those among whom they lived; separated from their loved ones on the auction block, experiencing the cruelty and the unmercifulness of a psychotic slave master, the slaves embraced the Christian faith and interpreted it to be a religion of compensation in the life to come for the ills which they had experienced here. The Christian faith was for the slaves a religion of reversals of conditions of the rich and poor, the proud and meek, of master and slave. It was this interpretation of the Christian faith which produced a body of songs which gave voice to all of the basic virtues of the Christian faith—faith, hope, love, courage, patience, forbearance, forgiveness, freedom, emancipation, liberation, victory. The black slaves took refuge in the Christian faith.[17]

The slave song and the sermon were primary means whereby

African slaves in America could experience God's abiding presence. These instruments of worship developed into ways of transmitting God's divine reality and the human possibility. Johnson wrote:

> The early preacher was primarily the preacher of the word. His messages were determined by the reality of death, the difficulties of life, and the saving word which he discovered in the Bible. His ultimate purpose was one of bringing healing and liberation to a despised and depressed people who were exposed to the vast ambiguities of life. He sought by the word of God to bring healing and liberation to the broken personhood of black men and women whose lives had been disrupted and degraded by slavery. . . . The black preacher stood midway between the inexhaustible storehouse of spiritual dynamics and the depleted lives of his black brothers and shouted, "Walk together, children, don't you get weary," or moaned, "There's a balm in Gilead."[18]

Worship is sanctuary in that it is an event in which God is present and the holiness of God's presence is made known. The brick and mortar of a building are transformed into a sacred setting. The song and the sermon empower African Americans to recognize God's possibilities in the next day's journey. Persons are invited to engage, with glad hearts, in the journey up the rough side of the mountain. Their energy is renewed for the experiences that come after. Their encounters with God become the pivotal points for what is to follow. Elements and patterns of African-American worship give definition to the sanctuary strategy of education.

The concern of the sanctuary strategy, like the concern of the story and exile strategies, is twofold. One, scripture is taught so that God's new order—an order of creation reconciled—is made known. Two, persons are invited to pattern their lives according to God's reconciled creation. Two of the distinctions between the sanctuary strategy and the story and exile strategies are the ways in which information is acquired and reconstructed.

Teaching scripture through the processes of the sanctuary strategy allows learners to take on the duties and privileges of membership in the church. The strategy inspires members to die and rise with Christ. It equips persons to view life with new meaning and purpose. Teaching scripture for sanctuary leads persons to the discovery of God's divine reality. It assists African Americans in seeing a life purpose in their daily activity, and that life purpose is made known in the living of their days.

The sanctuary strategy of education involves three phases: (1) identification of separation and alienation, (2) an orientation toward reconciliation, and (3) an invitation to incorporation. These phases enable persons to separate themselves from one way of living and become oriented and incorporated into a new and/or different way of life. Like the exile strategy, the movement toward sanctuary involves the creation and sustaining of harmonious relationships. But the sanctuary strategy extends beyond socialization to a faithful response to God. Sanctuary empowers persons to participate meaningfully in the Christian community of faith, including the experience of reconciliation with God and with one another.

PHASE 1: IDENTIFICATION OF SEPARATION AND ALIENATION

The task of this phase is to locate and describe with cultural specificity the ordinary experiences of life. Phase 1 does not assume that persons recognize how their daily experiences relate to the concerns of God. They must discover their life experiences as earthen vessels revealing the transcendent power and presence of God.

The task of the first phase in the sanctuary strategy is similar to the initial task of the two previous strategies. The distinctions rest in the acquiring, structuring, and restructuring of the information and experiences. The activity of making meaning is bound in and emerges from the ordering and patterning of experience and one's reflection on experience. Meaning does not exist in a vacuum; nor does it exist in chaos. The sanctuary strategy of education understands and makes use of worship as a patterned event for making meaning in the lives of learners. The nature of the rhythm, process, and structure of worship itself (or other patterned rituals) shapes the nature of the information and experience to be reflected on. Therefore, the initial task of the strategies is the same, but the outcome is different.

It is in the African-American experience (in the search for both personal and collective identity; in the communal quest for a corporate calling; and in the struggle for hope and healing amid chaos, conflict, and crime) that God's extraordinary grace emerges. During this phase the individual and cultural texts of African Americans are introduced and explored. Identifying the character of the African-American existence motivates people to learn and honors their experience as true.

PHASE 2: AN ORIENTATION TOWARD RECONCILIATION

The purpose of this phase is to unite the holy and the profane; to understand human existence in relation to the Source of all creation. The presentation and discussion of the scripture is offered in terms of the experience of God's reconciling activity in the world.

The function of this phase is to present information that may initiate a new or different structuring of reality. Scripture is the foundation for the church's understanding of God's first creation. The Word of God is also the church's source for recognizing God's work toward the fulfillment of the new creation. The restructuring of a person's world view may facilitate her or his faithful response. Through study of God's Word, persons come to know of God's meaning and purpose, hear the invitation to take up their cross and live after the example of Jesus Christ, and experience anew the Word living among them.

PHASE 3: AN INVITATION TO INCORPORATION

In the setting of the sanctuary, African Americans experience a culturally specific form of ritual. The ritual is known as worship, and it empowers persons to perceive God's presence. Worship enables us to overcome our alienation from God and one another and enriches our will to live under God's reign in the world. The ritual of worship functions to help a believer understand and order her or his life in a particular way.

In African tribes, rituals of initiation surround persons from birth to adulthood. This shows the importance of ritual to the life of the tribe. Alex Haley's *Roots* offers many examples. The following excerpt shows how a ritual shaped the self-understanding and the character of the people of Juffure. The story describes part of the ceremony of the birth initiation rite.

> Omoro then walked out before all of the assembled people of the village. Moving to his wife's side, he lifted up the infant and, as all watched, whispered three times into his son's ear the name he had chosen for him.

It was the first time the name had ever been spoken as this child's name, for Omoro's people felt that each human being should be the first to know who he was.

Out under the moon and the stars, alone with his son that eighth night, Omoro completed the naming ritual. Carrying little Kunta in his arms, he walked to the edge of the village, lifted his baby up with his face to the heavens, and said softly, "Fend killing dorong leh warrata ka iteh tee." (Behold—the only thing greater than yourself.)[19]

The function of initiation rituals in the traditioning processes of African culture is akin to the role and function of the ritual of worship for African Americans.

The sanctuary strategy for teaching scripture is effective because worship is central to the life of African-American congregations. Rituals were also significant for the ancestors of African Americans. The rituals of worship as experienced in African-American culture may not (and need not) take the same form as they do in African culture. But the role and function of ritual is the same.

The Strategy Applied

PHASE 1: IDENTIFICATION OF SEPARATION AND ALIENATION

Meeting the goals of this phase is accomplished through the presentation and reflection on a cultural text. The slave song "I've Got a Robe" is an example of an African-American cultural text that may be used in the setting of worship.

I've Got a Robe

I've got a robe, you've got a robe,
All of God's children got a robe
When I get to heaven goin' to put on my robe,
Goin' to shout all over God's heav'n.

Heav'n, heav'n,
Ev'rybody talkin' 'bout heav'n ain't goin' there,
Heav'n, heav'n,
Goin to shout all over God's heav'n.

I've got shoes, you've got shoes,
All of God's children got shoes.
When I get to heaven goin' to put on my shoes,
Goin' to shout all over God's heav'n.

Persons arrive at a learning experience accompanied by a history. They have reflected on and made sense of some of their experiences, but not all of them. This is true for both individuals and for groups. They also come with some understanding of God and the ministry and mission of the church of Jesus Christ.

The identification of separation and alienation phase allows the teacher to learn how much reflection has occurred. It includes assessing how well persons have processed traditional or cultural views and allows them to express their personal attitudes as well.

This phase points to the relevancy, value, and usefulness the subject has for the learners. A culturally specific text such as "I've Got a Robe" enables learners to make connections from the vantage point of prior knowledge.

Questions may include the following: What does the cultural text say? What do you suppose were the questions, concerns, hopes, or fears of the writer? Do you share any of those questions, concerns, hopes, or fears? Where does the text suggest that learners begin?

What other narratives, rituals, traditions, and symbols represent African Americans' experiences? For example, the ritual of Holy Communion is, in part, prominent in African-American congregations because it represents in symbol, song, and ritual God's power over destructive forces in society. What are rituals, symbols, and traditions of African-American communities that present the experiences of chaos and creation? For example, mothers bearing children out of wedlock, in many instances, highlights conditions of chaos and brokenness, while the extended family creates and presents new patterns and promises of reconciled relationships. What are ways and means by which the sacraments of baptism and Holy Communion can be used to present the story and experience of African Americans? Does the symbol of the cross have more than ornamental usage in your community? Is the altar used regularly as a special place in the congregation's worship of God? What is the community's tradition during the seasons of Lent? Pentecost? Advent?

PHASE 2: ORIENTATION TOWARD RECONCILIATION

In this phase the teacher and learners read and study the Word of God. The aim is to explore the scripture so that persons may know

God's Word with both head and heart. Many passages in the Bible evoke the imagery of God's new creation. Three examples from the Old Testament, the Gospel narratives, and Paul's letters are the story of Jacob and Esau (Genesis 27-33), the Prodigal Son (Luke 15:11-32), and Paul's letter to the Christians at Rome (Romans 5:1-11ff).

In the Old Testament, reconciliation is associated with redemption and righteousness. The term *reconciliation* involves the release of an item or person in exchange for some type of payment, the redemption of an inheritance, or the redemption of family members from servitude or difficulties. In reconciliation God restores, makes things new, and reconstitutes human disposition. Reconciliation is the result of an encounter with God which turns resistant hearts to God's way and will.

The New Testament writings claim that the potential for human redemption and reconciliation is made complete in Jesus Christ. The life of Christ presents a blueprint of God's intention for human co-existence with all creation. The death of Christ offers the atoning sacrifice for human rebellion against God's will and way. The resurrection of Christ extends to all the opportunity to claim their reconciliation with God. The reconciling event of the New Testament makes known God's matchless grace and unending mercy.

Thus, the purpose of this second phase in the sanctuary strategy is to make known God's intentions for creation and to lead persons to discover how to embrace God's reconciliation in behaviors and patterns of relations. The scripture is taught so that persons may become open and sensitive to God's activity and abiding presence in history and so that they may more fully understand and engage in Christian discipleship.

Reconciliation results in changed relationships between a person and God, other persons, and God's creation. The orientation is toward living a reconciled life becoming right with God. God makes this possible through the life, death, and resurrection of Jesus the Christ. The sanctuary strategy provides an occasion for learners to see from their souls, to hear with their hearts, to experience God's abiding presence, and to respond with their lives. This is an orientation toward reconciliation that brings about God's new creation.

Examples of questions for reflection may include the following. What was recorded in the scripture? How do you think the scripture accounts for and/or addresses your relationship with God?

Your relationship with others? Your response to God's created order?

How may the scriptures' central messages be used to develop other rituals, traditions, and symbols that possess the vitality to shape participants' views and future? Do the parables and narratives of scripture, rituals, traditions, and symbols of the community inform the personal and communal identity of members?

PHASE 3: AN INVITATION TO INCORPORATION

Phase 3 extends to learners an opportunity and responsibility to share in acts that give definition and support to the Christian way of life. Learners are invited to participate in the rituals and traditions of the church that transform its identity and encourage their faithful participation. They are sustained by God's promise that God will be with them forever.

The learner moves from passive to active participation in the faith community. She or he is called upon in daily life to re-enact rituals and to give allegiance to the traditions and symbols of Christian faith. But the goal goes beyond socialization as good Christian citizens to rebirth through one's awareness of living in the presence and with the power of God. The African-American expression "we had church" refers to the Holy One's self-disclosure and the group's awareness of existence before the Holy One. Examples of the group's reaction to this presence may include a response to invitations to baptism, confirmation, or Holy Communion. Or the reaction may be embracing in common situations terms such as "disciple of Christ" or "people of the cross."

The view that a person does not become fully human until she or he has ordered her or his life in a particular manner is common to many African tribes. Ritual functions as a means of expressing the pattern of life desired. The ceremonies and traditions encourage allegiance to patterns that are believed to correspond with divine reality. Ceremonies and rituals of initiation are a primary way to share a tribe's or a culture's sense of meaning, order, and purpose.

Teaching scripture by means of rituals and traditioning processes is a way to introduce persons to the faith community. When a community recalls experiences from its past, the recollection incorporates anew that past in its present life. The community shares its language and the meaning of its symbols with persons who do not know them. The recollection invites persons who are unfamiliar with the community's heritage to claim that heritage for themselves. This becomes a significant moment for the community and for the learner. Rituals and traditions remind a community of its view of life, and practicing the rituals and traditions incorporates outsiders into community.

The invitation to incorporation phase gives learners a chance to engage the scriptures in ways that may shape and transform their identity. Teaching scripture in this manner may provide cohesion and continuity between African-American congregations and the communities in which they exist. Presenting and re-enacting the scripture through rituals and traditions of incorporation may offer African Americans a standard for re-interpretation and refinement of an African-American theology in light of an everchanging situation.

Participation in learning scripture through the community's rituals and traditions enables a person to share in creative activity, and it allows for the presentation and reflection of both the existing order and God's new and/or intended order of creation. Community rituals that teach the scripture include baptism, Holy Communion, and African-American rites of Kwaanza and Orieta.

Questions that focus on the issue include, What relevancy do the ritual and the traditioning processes have to the ongoing life of the congregation? In times of crisis, do persons call the congregation to the altar for prayer? Is Holy Communion used at times other than the predetermined, routine times?

Biblical and theological themes abound. These include scripture passages that focus on rebirth, reconciliation, redemption, regeneration, eschatology, and salvation. The Wesleyan teachings of prevenient, justifying, and sanctifying grace are examples of church doctrines that may be used with the strategy.

The general theme of separation and incorporation may help to identify and explore personal concerns appropriate for the strategy. Personal or communal issues related to life passages and transition points have currency for these teaching and learning processes. These life changes may include periods of biological, psychological, vocational, and/or sociological transition. For example, traditions for incorporating a newborn child into the community or celebrating a person's life in the community can also meaningfully teach the scripture.

Conclusion

The sanctuary strategy of education has the teaching of scripture as its primary goal. Teaching scripture for sanctuary through the use of ritual empowers persons with the language, stories, and traditions of the Christian faith to respond to the cries of life. Using this method of teaching recalls for the Christian community God's will for humankind. It prepares learners to recognize God's presence in their midst, and it challenges persons to come to know God's reality.

CHAPTER 4
The Exodus Strategy of Education

When he came to Nazareth, where he had been brought up, he went to the synagogue on the sabbath day, as was his custom. He stood up to read, and the scroll of the prophet Isaiah was given to him. He unrolled the scroll and found the place where it was written:

"The Spirit of the Lord is upon me, because he has anointed me to bring good news to the poor. He has sent me to proclaim release to the captives and recovery of sight to the blind, to let the oppressed go free, to proclaim the year of the Lord's favor."

And he rolled up the scroll, gave it back to the attendant, and sat down. The eyes of all in the synagogue were fixed on him. Then he began to say to them, "Today this scripture has been fulfilled in your hearing" (Luke 4:16-21).

Teaching Scripture and the Metaphor of Exodus

Teaching scripture is the fundamental task of Christian education. Teaching scripture enriches the lives of teachers and learners with understandings of the church's ministry and mission. Teaching scripture paints the vision of God upon the canvasses of human hearts. It couches in human terms the hope of heaven.

The metaphor of exodus is the paradigm of this educational strategy for teaching scripture. The exodus was primary to the life of ancient Israel and throughout history remains central to their sense of character and purpose. Israel's exodus from Egypt formed the community. It led them to know the God of creation as an agent of liberation in human affairs. The exodus was (and continues to be) Israel's "calling card." Their vocation and mission in life are grounded in the historical experience of their freedom from Pharaoh in search of the Promised Land.

The narratives of the patriarchs tell about the Hebrews going to Egypt to avoid the famine of Caanan. While in Egypt, their hardship turned into heartache. "So that the Egyptians came to dread the Israelites. The Egyptians became ruthless in imposing tasks on the Israelites, and made their lives bitter with hard service in mortar and brick and in every kind of field labor. They were ruthless in all the tasks that they imposed on them" (Exodus 1:12*b*-14). Israel had become an oppressed people in Egypt. They were made the slaves of the power elite. They were held captive and sentenced to a lifetime of meaningless servitude.

During the thirtieth century B.C., when Pharaoh Rameses II (leader of the nineteenth dynasty) was ruler of Egypt, the plight of the Hebrews came to an end. The bonds of their servitude were broken. There would be no more days of rigorous work and nights of bitter tears. Held captive by the hands of the Egyptians, they were set free by the hand of God from the labors of the Egyptian task masters. They were set free to live in the land of promise. They were freed from a life of worthlessness to become a people of God.

Like the captivity and oppression of the Israelites, the African-American experience has been an experience of captivity and oppression. Uprooted from their native soil, Africans were set in shackles to sail on slave ships. The African-American plight in the United States has been an excursion on the freeway of inequality. We have walked on the roadways of racism. We have been made to live on the avenues of injustice. African Americans have been victims of systemic oppression. But the Exodus narrative gives assurance that right is stronger than might and "that truth crushed to earth will rise again."

African Americans have heard and used the exodus story as a song of hope. The African slaves inherited the exodus story from the biblical tradition, and through that story the God of life and liberation met the slaves' immediate needs. The exodus of the Israelites from the dominion of Pharaoh has existential relevancy for the African-American community. The story is an oasis of hope amid deserts of hopelessness.

African-American communities continue to be surrounded by the parched lands of oppression, injustice, and inequality. The exodus story remains a wellspring for action. The prominence of racism in America led African Americans to claim help from the Liberator who acts in human history. The contemporary faces of human suffering in the world beckon Christians to work and witness on the side of God today.

The exodus strategy of education uses sociopolitical analysis as the primary process for teaching scripture. The process leads learners to discover underlying issues and values and their relationship to existing situations, norms, and policies. Liberation and justice are major themes. A significant challenge of the strategy is to teach scripture so that learners may discover and explore the relationship between individual problems and public life. The aim of the exodus strategy includes the support and/or development of public policies and strategies that ensure a just and equitable society.

Principles and policies that support life and health are consistent with doing God's will. Performing acts of love, justice, and service is working the will of God. Teaching scripture cannot be divorced from doing God's will any more than life can be separated from breathing or Christ's disciples disconnected from the Breath of Life. A faithful teaching of the scripture inspires teachers and learners to discover God's presence in ministry with others. Faithful acts of witness and service are informed and nurtured by the Word of God.

The Strategy

Parallels between African-American experiences and that of the ancient Hebrews are the basis for the exodus strategy of education. The African-American experience of contradiction has greatly influenced the African Americans' construction of identity, reality, and relationships. C. Eric Lincoln wrote of the experience in terms of the "corporate contradiction."

> The most obvious—and the only official—sources of religious indoctrination for the slaves were the white preachers and exhorters who shared as a matter of course the prevailing presumptions of the slaveowners. The other source, which came to be called the Invisible Church, represented the slaves' effort to meet God on their own. . . . Christianity taught to black people began with the injunction "servants, obey your master," and concluded with the warning: "He that knoweth the will of the master and doeth it not will be beaten with many stripes."[20]

Throughout the journey in North America, African Americans have had to make sense of the distinctions between the words and the actions of European Americans. For example, the creed of the American government, the constitution, says that all people are created equal. Yet an African American, then called "slave, boy, girl, or nigger," was only three-fifths of a person. Salvation rescued one from the pits of separation from every condition, *except* from the condition of slavery and bondage. "Protestant leaders developed not only the highest form of chattel slavery ever known to human-kind; they also desired the baptism of all those who were enslaved. They saw no contradiction between these two actions."[21] For African-American slaves, both religious and civil experiences of contradiction were present in their construction of identity, reality, and relationships. (Read again "We Wear the Mask," page xii.)

African-American experiences of power and powerlessness shaped their view and participation in history. One of the major distinctions between African-American and European and Ger-manic ethnic groups in the United States is the African Americans' lack of systemic, institutional, and structural power and/or access to power. Even within the church African Americans are generally without the systemic power to effect change.

> The Black Church's traditional reluctance to place itself in direct opposi-tion to the white power structure grew partly out of the hard lessons it learned from experience, both actual and vicarious. Myth and conven-tion so confused this experience that objective analysis was impossible in most cases. The result was a mystical invulnerability for all whites as a class, before which all Blacks stood helplessly exposed. Pushed to its logical conclusions, this meant that, ultimately, life itself depended upon the white man's goodwill, his charitableness, and his forbearance.[22]

In contrast to the lack of systemic, institutional, and structural power, we African Americans have claimed our grace for accessing the power and presence of God. By means of storytelling, music, prayers, preaching, and disciplines of service and witness, we have opened ourselves to the good whose power is not confined to the systems, structures, and institutions of the earth.

In spite of experiences of contradiction and powerlessness, African Americans have been agents of change. Our witness to the liberating God has challenged the social and economic systems of Western culture. Our claim of Jesus Christ's transforming power has altered the inhumanity we once encountered. And our struggle to confront conditions of inequality has nurtured our growth in Chris-tian faith.

Four other consequences occur from teaching scripture by use of the exodus strategy. One is unique to the exodus educational method. Three are similar to the intentions of the other strategies. First, relationships are recognized that empower teachers and learners to discover other perspectives of reality. For example, through sociopolitical analysis, relationships between personal and social issues are connected. Persons discover links between values and public policies. And biblical faith informs strategies that move toward just and right action.

Second, the scripture is taught. The exodus strategy is grounded in the study of God's Word. Reading and reflecting on the scripture provides a foundation for learners to perform acts of service and witness to the Christ of the New Jerusalem. The study of the scripture is intentionally and inseparably connected to the personal and social activity of God's presence and power.

Third, the exodus strategy nurtures persons in their growth in faith. It empowers them to become agents of change in the work of God. Their growth in faith includes acts of service and witness on behalf of Christ. The exodus strategy's second purpose focuses on socializing learners into a Christian identity, a Christian view of life, and a Christian response to the concerns of life. Persons are informed and inspired to engage in the mission and ministry of Christ.

Fourth, the exodus strategy of education is both personally and socially transformational. The strategy understands that personal and social realms of existence are inextricably bound together. Personal piety that falls short of wrestling with social transformation is not akin to Christ—neither is social transformation that neglects to challenge and invite learners to claim Jesus as Savior and Lord of their life. By inspiring persons with courage to give witness to the reign of God on earth, the transforming power of God in Christ is at work for personal and social redemption.

Faith without works is dead, and action without understanding is meaningless. Study of the scripture with no witness and service is less than a faithful response to the Lord of life. Acts of witness and service without a biblical frame of reference are void of Christian meaning and purpose. Without the study of scripture and placement of acts of witness and service in the community of faith, social witness becomes civil service.

The exodus strategy gives public witness to God's will. It equips persons to address the systems, structures, and policies that regulate human relationships. It intends to develop systems, structures, and policies that may correspond to God's intent. But the strategy places acts of witness and service in relationship with the scripture so that learners may know that their witness is in response to the initiating activity of God. In the exodus strategy God's Word moves learners toward participation in God's reign.

The exodus strategy works to constructively influence the relationship between knowing the scripture and responding with acts of love and service. The strategy challenges two assumptions. The first concerns the relative power of knowledge. It is not necessarily true that if persons know the scripture, the content of the Christian tradition, and their denominational heritage, they will live according to that information. Informing the intellect does not automatically motivate the will to act.

The second assumption that is challenged concerns the difference between doing good and doing the work of Christ. Persons who perform acts of love and service do not necessarily share Christian views about the importance of the acts. They may perform acts of service for reasons other than God's initiating acts of love and grace.

The exodus strategy works to motivate learners to act. The strategy differs from the previous strategies in that its primary processes are analytical and its intent is to inform public policy. If the strategy has a bias, it is toward informed, strategic action. By clarifying the issues and the agents involved, persons gain encouragement for the task of service to the neighbors of God. The strategy helps learners explore possibilities for a more equitable environment. It moves learners to identify other persons and groups who may be enlisted to join them on the journey toward a more just society. It encourages learners to take responsibility for embracing a life of shalom in the world.

The exodus strategy involves a four-step process that influences the selection of content and the acquisition of related information from memory toward the reconstruction of a faithful response.

Step 1: The strategy begins with a descriptive analysis of what is occurring in the sociopolitical environment of the learners. It does this through the presentation and reflection of the African-American experience as the cultural text. This step in the educational process if referred to as "The Orientation."

Step 2: "Action Formulation." This begins with the teaching and study of the scripture in conversation with the African-American experience. Learners are given opportunity to explore and discover how scripture may become integrated and applied to particular situations. The scripture serves to lead learners toward the construction of creative alternatives to life as it is known at present.

Step 3: "The Exodus." This step is an occasion for learners to do and participate in God's promises. Learners are provided opportunity to refine and carry out their creative response in the world. The learner's construction of a creative alternative is applied to his or her personal-public problem. This step supports the transfer of information from memory to active conscience, and from working conscience to long-term memory.

Step 4: "Revising the Witness." This step includes three tasks: reflecting on the witness, revising the action formulation, and inspiring and supporting God's people for a long-term commitment.

The Strategy Applied

Because the exodus strategy may be used to address a wide variety of concerns, a specific example will not be given. Rather, an outline of the process will be presented along with questions used to guide learners in their use of the strategy. Information to assist a group's study/action may come from many sources, such as the public library, magazines, journals, government documents, as well as Bible helps and commentaries.

STEP 1. THE ORIENTATION

The purpose is to locate the concern in the life experience of the learners. Beginning at this point allows learners to engage in learning processes with a connection to their experience. Starting here also gives validation to the African-American experience.

This phase begins with an introduction of an issue from the perspective of the African-American experience, an action similar to the first step of the story strategy in that the cultural text may emerge from the writings of African Americans, such as poetry, short stories, newspaper articles, or books written by and about African Americans. Or the cultural text may come from the arts, including music, photography, and African-American drama.

This step differs from the story strategy in that all processes are bound by the patterns and processes used. As relationships are recognized between personal and public issues and as values that support and/or conflict with one's view of reality are made known, the interaction of the information results in different insights gained. The ways and means in which information is grouped and presented result in different messages sent and perceived.

From the introduction learners move to explore the issue broadly. Examination of the concern includes a view of the social, political, and economic context. The aim is to gain a broad, clear picture about the situation. The questions below provide an approach to this task.

1. What is a problem with which you struggle?
2. In what ways have you and others experienced this problem before?
3. Where do persons with this problem do things together?
4. How does this problem continue to occur?
5. Who makes decisions about the ways the concern is addressed?
6. What agencies and institutions claim to address the problem identified?
7. Who benefits from the decisions that are made?
8. Who pays the cost for the implementation of the decisions?

STEP 2. ACTION FORMULATION

This phase begins with a study of the scripture and moves toward the development of a strategy. First, persons are invited to examine the scripture to gain insight and inspiration for participating in the concerns of God. Learners then are led to imagine alternative futures that move the community toward a more just and loving realization of the City of God in the world.

By studying scripture, learners prepare themselves to make and take responsible action. The scripture is the primary resource of faith for the Christian learner. For Christians, learning takes place in the context of the Christian community. This includes taking into account the Christian community's previous interpretations and responses as Christians read and develop their faithful acts of witness and service. Study of the scripture illuminates past witnesses of faith. Teaching scripture also opens the windows of possibility into the future. The questions that follow may help persons in their response to the scripture.

1. What is recorded in the scripture?
2. What are similarities and tensions between the biblical character's personal problem(s) and the biblical community's public beliefs and ways of living?
3. How do the biblical community's values support and conflict with the biblical writer's understanding of God's intent?
4. According to the biblical author, what are answers and solutions to the biblical community's personal-public problem?
5. What new images and possibilities do you see for the biblical community's life together?
6. What behaviors and actions does the above discussion challenge you to embrace?

The primary distinction between this process of Bible reflection and that of the other strategies may be understood by an analogy from chemistry. Content affects process, and process affects product. Different products come into being when different chemical elements (content) are mixed together. For example, two molecules of hydrogen and one molecule of oxygen interact and become water. If the one molecule of oxygen is omitted from the compound and/or replaced with any other molecule, water will not be the consequence of the reaction. When the content is changed, the process of mixing is changed as well. For example, the nature of the reaction process is altered when oxygen is not an ingredient of the chemical process because of oxygen's combustive properties. So too does the learner come to a different understanding of scripture when the Bible is in one hand and the daily newspaper or an analysis of a problem is in the other hand.

STEP 3. THE EXODUS

Following scripture study, learners may begin to form their response and to integrate and claim allegiance to God in response to the Word of God. This enables learners to perform acts of witness and service in light of specific experiences and life concerns. The following questions may assist learners toward integration and application of the scripture to particular life concerns.

1. What beliefs and understandings are important?
2. What public policies, practices, and perspectives can and must be addressed to erase the personal problem?
3. Who are the persons, agencies, and institutions that are to join in conversation in order to address the systemic nature of the personal problem?
4. How are persons to organize in order to challenge policies and practices so that a more just and equitable way of life may come into being?
5. In what way(s) may the worship and liturgy of the congregation inform the vision and support these actions?
6. How will the group invite, encourage, and enlist others to know and participate in the vision?

The exodus step invites and encourages learners to move from the place of study and preparation to the laboratory of life "where the rubber meets the road." The experience of inhumanity, injustice, and inequality among African Americans does not allow learners to perform acts of justice only inside the walls of the church house. If Christians are to present a viable witness to God on behalf of the Lord of the resurrection, then action must accompany proclamation.

Teaching scripture in order to develop a more just society is necessary. It allows Christian learners to state clearly their understandings and intent. And it offers the possibility for enlisting others to join in the cause of God. But the learning and worshiping community is to become the witnessing community as well.

Teaching scripture effectively moves learners to carry the vision of God's Word into their world. It challenges them to be responsive to the needs of the human community. It leads learners to exit from the halls of inhumanity and to enter the land of promise. Teaching scripture makes it possible to claim Christ's example as servant-leader as their way in the world, too.

STEP 4. REVISING THE WITNESS

The exodus strategy emerges from conflicts around the values persons uphold. What persons understand to be important shapes the ways in which they live. Conflict arises when persons differ in what they believe is important, and the resulting conflict may lead to a chasm in the fabric of the human community if left unattended.

The exodus strategy recognizes that Christian teachers and learners are responsible for going beyond the conflict resulting from the pursuit of a more just society. Learners need to be taught how to live with those with whom they disagree. The scripture must be taught in its fullness. Persons need to learn how to abhor acts of injustice and still love the one who acts.

A faithful witness needs to be revised as the situation changes. Persons respond to experiences either actively or passively, and conditions change for better or worse. Because of this continuous change, the formulation of an effective strategy is flexible. Learners uphold the values of the Christian community, yet remain open to new ways and means of realizing equity and justice for all.

A faithful witness calls for reflection on acts performed on behalf of the God of love and mercy. The exodus strategy of education teaches scripture and engages learners in struggles for a more just and loving community so that persons and communities are transformed. Questions to be considered at this phase may include those below.

1. What is the present experience? In what ways is the experience different now than it was before the group's action?
2. What limitations and opportunities were realized as a result of the action taken and the proposals, policies, and programs developed?
3. How have the persons who experienced injustices previously benefited from the group's response(s)?
4. In what way(s) are persons who experienced inequities before now empowered to determine their own course of action?

Conclusion

The scripture is taught in the context of particular cultures. The experiences and traditions of particular cultures must not be discounted, but upheld. Then learners become empowered to perform acts of service and witness on behalf of the Lord of the church. When God's Word is made known through the experience of learners, their lives are ennobled to uphold the sacredness of God's creation.

The scripture is taught so that persons become moved to do God's will. Teaching scripture faithfully always includes an invitation to respond to God. Teaching scripture in order to merely possess accurate information is not only insufficient; it is heresy. The scriptures are taught so that persons may realize God's will and presence and live in love and justice with all of God's creation.

The Bible and the church's views of its meanings call Christians to responsible participation in setting things right. Debate over the course of action does not dismiss the obligation to address unjust, inhumane, and oppressive conditions. The need to develop and implement strategies to set things right does call teachers and learners of the church to engage in the human task of risking self and trusting the promises of God.

On one hand, every situation of life that calls for a decision is an occasion for the use of the strategy. On the other hand, the life issues that call for decisions to be made are related to the social context of human existence. Oppressed people, segregated societies, and others who live as victims of sin experience reality as a social affair. Yet the reality of inequity is not ordained by God. In teaching the scripture the teachers and learners must say no in word and action to every act that destroys human dignity and yes to strategies that empower persons to translate Christian understandings into action.

The exodus strategy of education is concerned with educating disciples of Christ for social responsibility. This strategy views the social responsibility of Christian education as inseparable from personal responsibility. The Christian understanding of God's will and purpose, as made known through the life, death, and resurrection of Jesus Christ, does not isolate or segregate individuals from their relationship to the social world. Rather, Christian faith asserts that the meaning of humanness implies that persons are social beings.

PART II

CHAPTER 5
TEACHING SCRIPTURE WITH CULTURAL SPECIFICITY

Why is it necessary for teaching strategies to give attention to distinctive characteristics of racial ethnic groups? Why must approaches that teach the scripture recognize and make use of African-American cultural patterns of behavior and learning? Can scripture be taught in ways that uphold both the Christian tradition and the life experiences of a particular culture? How may a community embrace its historical experience and express its oneness in Christ with other communities? Why is it important to use culturally specific teaching and learning strategies for teaching Christian faith? How may teachers determine and transmit the Christian faith and heritage in and to society today?

Shifts in Christian Education Purposes in United States Culture

Christian education has had different emphases through the years, and all of them were influenced by culture. Christian education for African Americans began during the early 1600s. Its intent was to provide instruction in reading and Christian faith to African slaves. They received instruction, embraced the ideals that were taught, and claimed their conversion. They were baptized into Christianity. But when questions were raised about the effect of baptism on the status of the slave, problems emerged. This situation caused Christians and slave masters to redefine the purpose and role of religious instruction in relation to slavery.

Responses to questions about the aim and role of religious education came from many quarters. In 1701, The Society for the Propagation of the Gospel in Foreign Parts sent Englishman Samuel Thomas to evangelize and educate African slaves in South Carolina. The Society of Friends (commonly known as Quakers) believed in the Africans' self-worth, taught them, and argued against the institution of slavery. The London Society for the Promotion of Religious Knowledge among the Poor, led by the Presbyterian Samuel Davies, offered another proposal. They announced that the aim of religious instruction was to prepare slaves for freedom and a life of moral integrity. The Moravians carried out religious education in biracial settings. The environment supported their belief that "Jews and Gentiles, slave or free," were one in Christ. The Methodists and Baptists provided religious education for the African slaves too, but they did so in segregated settings. And the context of their religious teachings allowed them to vacillate on the purposes of Christian teachings for Africans in a new land.[23]

The Sunday school movement that emerged from leadership within the United States continued the shifts in the purposes of religious education. It was initiated by a newspaper philanthropist, Robert Raikes. Raikes was motivated to explore ways and means by which persons could be deterred from criminal activity. He believed that poverty and ignorance were root causes that led persons to share in criminal acts. Raikes responded by starting schools on Sundays to assist in shaping persons' moral character.

From this beginning the Sunday school shifted its audience and its purposes.

> From the mid-1820's until the Civil War, it appears that the Sunday school existed with two objectives. . . . William Alcott . . . argued that the 'best children of our best and most pious families' attend Sunday school. . . . James Alexander . . . called Sunday schools 'the best means yet devised for the rapid and successful instruction and salvation for the multitudes who are perishing for lack of knowledge.' This dual purpose continued in the minds of some proponents until the 1860's.[24]

From this moment onward, the Sunday school would wrestle with the tension between its purposes of mission and its obligation to serve the institutional church. Eventually, more attention would be given to addressing the concerns of church members than to reaching the impoverished and those who lacked knowledge with the message of the gospel.

Shifts in Christian Education Processes in United States Culture

The processes of Christian education changed just as its purposes did. Christian education processes have taken on various forms and patterns and present the Christian faith tradition in the context of specific cultures, also.

The processes of translation[25] and adaptation are commonly used to teach the scripture and to construct a culture's understandings of God. Processes of translation involve a twofold task. (See Robert J. Schreiter, *Constructing Local Theologies,* in Bibliography.)

First, the translation process sets out to determine "the bottom line," the universal truth, the eternal principle. After the first task has been successfully completed, the translation process begins its second task, that of interpreting the eternal truth for a new situation. The translation approach is a common process of Christian education for African-American congregations.

Two strengths of the translation process are evident. One, it is an expedient process for Christian education. It offers an immediate response to crises or opportunities in different cultures. Two, the process supports and promotes past traditions of the Christian faith. It assumes that the church's traditions are connected with the culture in which it operates.

Three weaknesses are associated with the translation process and are located in the assumptions surrounding the process. First, the process assumes that a culture's patterns and ethos can be quickly detected and responded to. Second, it assumes that parallel situations readily exist in different cultures. Third, the translation approach oversimplifies the process of teaching scripture. In search of the fundamental principle, it assumes that universal truths are inherently singular. Translation processes negate the relationship of truth and context and the role of context in shaping truth.

A second kind of process involved in Christian education is the process of adaptation. The process of adaptation uses the experiences and traditions of one culture but attempts to formulate these in the constructs and philosophical designs of another culture. An analogy of this process is that of a camera lens taking a picture. The picture allows a culture's experience to be presented. However, inasmuch as the lens includes some object(s) and excludes other objects from the picture, the lens is a vehicle for shaping what view of reality is presented. All interpretations are dependent upon a picture or view of experience.

At least two strengths are associated with adaptation processes of Christian education. One, the processes allow for dialogue and discussion between cultures. By seeking common frames of reference, adaptation processes provide structures for conversation. Two, the processes raise the level of exposure pertaining to the cultural text.

Two weaknesses are also associated, however, with adaptation processes. They continue to speak from the vantage point of the majority or dominant culture, and they impose the dominant world view on the existential realities of other cultures. As the photographer with her camera determines what will be in the picture, so too does a culture with the instrument of the adaptation process determine the experience for reflection.

The purposes and processes of Christian education are embedded in particular cultures. They represent the faith tradition and the cultural ethos, patterns of relating, and ways of being in the world. The purposes and processes of Christian education articulate Christian faith, mirror the beliefs and customs of specific cultures, and reinforce and are reinforced by the structures of the culture in which they function. This reality is not inevitable, but it seems so. It does not have to be, yet it is.

> Christendom has often achieved apparent success by ignoring the precepts of its founder. The church, as an organization interested in self-preservation and in the gain of power, has sometimes found the counsel of the Cross quite as inexpedient as have national and economic groups faced with such issues as war, slavery, and social inequality. The church has allied itself to "power and prestige" rather than the demands of the Gospel. Christianity "has become part and parcel of the world, one social institution alongside many others, a phase of the total civilization more frequently conditioned by other cultural tendencies than conditioning them."[26]

Representing the Christian faith in the context of specific cultures is not necessarily destructive or evil, although it is limiting. It is destructive and evil when the purposes and processes of Christian education are dominated by one culture's perspective. It is destructive and evil when one culture determines the purposes and processes for teaching and learning for every culture. Inevitably the culture that determines what will be taught, how it will be taught, and how it will be made available to the public is the dominant culture.

Causes for Distinctions
Among African-American Culture

Culture is the container and agent of a society's beliefs and norms. It holds the experiences of a community in its rituals and customs. A society's culture transmits its values and beliefs through its religious ethos, patterns of association, and relationships. Culture is conserved by the laws and norms of the community. It is communicated through language, dance, and literature. "Culture or civilization, taken in its wide ethnographic sense, is that complex whole which includes knowledge, belief, art, morals, law, custom, and any other capabilities and habits acquired by man as a member of society."[27]

Culture has various functions within a society or group. Culture regulates the behavior of the members through laws and customs. It supports and reinforces the values and norms of a society by granting permission and assigning condemnation. It provides for the existence of structures within society and makes possible the continuity of relationships.

Michael Apple provides an example of how culture functions in settings where the tasks of education are at work. Apple writes: "The choice of particular content and ways of approaching it in schools is related both to existing relations of domination and to struggle to alter these relations. . . . Though the ties that link curricula to the inequalities and social struggles of our social formation are very complicated . . . nevertheless, the social relations exist.[28]

The same is true for Christian education. Culture influences the choices that determine what information will be included and excluded for teaching and learning. The teachings and learnings of Christian education are contained in and carried through the values, customs, norms, and social arrangements of the church. And the repetitive nature of the culture perpetuates both the possibilities and limitations created by the culture. Culture is not inherited; it is learned and acquired.

The experience of African Americans in the United States illustrates how their cultural distinctiveness emerged. Concern about what makes the African-American personality distinct directs attention to three interrelated factors. All three factors relate to the historical experiences of African Americans. The factors center around retention, multiple worldviews, and group arrangements based on the exchange of goods and services.

Retention refers to the fact that neither African nor the African-American personality and culture was destroyed totally by the experiences of captivity or slavery or racism.

A factor that often facilitated the retention of the African orientation was the particular region's physical features. And the slaves' accessibility to Western indoctrination was probably directly related to the degree of the retention of the African orientation. The rigidly enforced isolation of blacks allowed New World Africans to retain their definition (orientation). Thus, the oppressive system of slavery indirectly encouraged the retention, rather than the destruction, of the Africa philosophical orientation.[29]

Janice Hale-Benson, in her book *Black Children: Their Roots, Culture, and Learning Styles,* agrees with this view. Hale-Benson refers to the experience of retention as the "survivalist view" of African-American culture. The survivalist view opposes the propositions that every vestige of culture was destroyed during slavery. The survivalist perspective challenges the notion that the primary task of African Americans is to make a "contribution" to Western civilization. The task of African Americans is not to become "a credit to their race." Multiple cultures do exist within the United States, and the distinctiveness of their culture does not necessarily make them deficient.

Multiple worldviews also characterize the development of African Americans' distinct culture. Hale-Benson writes:

> The autonomous Black culture is an elusive entity. In one context, it may come clearly to the fore; in the next, one wonders if one sees anything that other Americans would not do. . . . One needs a conceptual framework where the possibility is recognized that an individual can have more than one culture in his repertoire, that he can switch between these cultures quickly and that he can drift between them over a longer period.[30]

Patterns of relationships are a third expression of culture. Those with whom persons do and do not interact, the roles persons exhibit in their relationships, and the relations and conditions among groups express distinctions within and among cultures. Examples of the various conditions of relating may be seen clearly in the area of economics as well as Christian education.

African Americans are more inclined to be employees than employers.[31] They are buyers rather than sellers. They are more often consumers rather than owners. When African Americans interact with European Americans in the exchange of goods and services, they do so from an unequal position of power and strength. The inequality of their economic position conditions both their perception of themselves and their perception of the seller. The position from which lenders or sellers work influences their perceptions of themselves and of the buyer, too. And perceptions shape human behavior. Even though there are exceptions, these ways of relating represent the norm.

The same patterns exist in the realm of education—even Christian education. African Americans are more inclined to be receivers of information than givers. They are more often purchasers of curriculum than producers. When their history is told and their experience interpreted, it is commonly told *about* them rather than *from* them. These realities also influence the character of relationships and interactions. And both the realities and the relationships lead to distinctions among racial ethnic cultures.

Transforming Nature of Christian Education

The purposes and processes of Christian education need to rise to new possibilities and overcome old boundaries. Responsible Christian education initiates its own critique and reconstruction. It challenges bankrupt understandings while affirming truth that has currency for Christians in particular times and places.

For example, Christian education once assumed that American culture was inherently consistent with Christian ideals. A major function was then to teach in order to support the republic and democracy. This assumption has had to be challenged and enlarged. Christianity may include elements that are consistent with the democratic ideal; however, Christianity is in no way limited to current or ideal practices of democracy. The character of Christian education has to allow for its own evaluation. These older assumptions about culture and Christian education have lost much of their credibility. Christian education has had to reconstruct its mission, strategies, and processes in the light of new knowledge. It has had to become more truly Christian (and democratic) by allowing for greater participation from the plurality of God's people.

Christian education that is responsive to the plurality of God's people has one eye on God's immanence in history and the other eye on God's transcendence in eternity. The eye of history knows of God's nearness. The eye of eternity acknowledges that God is beyond. The eye of history experiences God in particular times and places. The eye of eternity points to understandings yet to unfold. The eye of eternity envisions that "it does not yet appear what we shall be" (1 John 3:2, KJV). Yet it has glanced at the future and believes that "We'll Understand It Better By and By." The eye of history recognizes the "God of our weary years, God of our silent tears, thou who hast brought us thus far on the way."[32]

The purposes and processes of Christian education, if these are to be faithful to its own teachings, must influence and be affected by God's presence within culture and by God's existence beyond culture. By understanding and upholding God's immanence and transcendence, Christian education embraces three values. (1) It allows the Christian community to embrace its diversity while affirming a sense of unity in Christ; (2) it makes possible the respect for every culture's experiences and heritages: and (3) it embraces more fully than otherwise the transformative nature of Christian faith.

Educating to Embrace Diversity

The purposes and processes of Christian education are important and necessary. Yet the purposes and processes are not to negate the culture of persons for whom they are intended. Christian education must allow for continuity and change. It must claim Christian faith as the foundation that gives it its ultimate shape and character. Christian education must allow for increasing numbers of persons with cultural differences to study the scripture and encounter the God of all creation in light of their particular experience.

Christian education that is located in understandings of God's immanence and transcendence provides for the existence of diversity within the unity of Christ. Christian views of God affirm God's diverse character. God is absolutely independent, yet is moved by the cries of victims. God in Christ takes on the human blood and flesh but remains wholly other. God is human and divine. The absolute nature of God's unchanging character is that God is forever changing. God's character is diverse.

Persons and cultures are diverse, too. Cultural diversity is a reality. To approach another person or people only from the stance of similarities negates their human experience. When the church does not provide for cultural diversity, it dismembers the Body of Christ.

For too long Christian education has acted as though "unity in Christ" meant uniformity rather than completeness or wholeness. This view of unity in Christ has led to and supported sameness and homogeneity in purpose, processes, and approaches. It has accounted for a changeless posture in the face of changing times and conditions.

Many places in society are more representative of American cultural diversity than the congregations in which Christian education occurs. Training centers in the workplace are just one example. When unity in Christ is understood as uniformity in what is to be taught (content), how it is to be taught (process), where it is to be taught (settings), and why it is taught (purpose), then Christian education is inhibited from becoming culturally specific. Thus, all peoples of God's creation are kept from becoming truly human. Respect for the experiences and traditions of all cultures is needed. Validating the cultural worldviews of all minority and oppressed peoples is imperative.

When Christian education upholds the immanence and transcendence of God, it is empowered to critique its weaknesses and to reconstruct its assumptions and responses. Understanding unity in Christ as completeness and wholeness challenges Christian education to answer questions. Who is missing from the teaching/learning experience? Who is setting the agenda? Who is determining the needs and the adequate response? What is being taught (content)? What are the intended objectives (purpose)? What are the strategies and approaches used (processes of selection and acquisition, and reconstruction)? Whose experience is acknowledged/discounted (motivation)?

The character of education that is Christian demands that it become concerned with the whole family of God. Unity in Christ as wholeness leads Christian education to explore and discover culturally diverse strategies so that persons may participate in and experience their cultural identity as an identity shaped in the fullness of God.

Educating to Respect Heritages

When Christian education is located in understandings of God's immanence and transcendence, then it becomes possible to respect every culture's experiences and heritage. The immanance and transcendence of God suggest that God holds all humanity and all of creation in holy regard. God's nearness is acknowledged in that God responds to human need within the context of every culture. God's independence is preserved through understanding that no culture can claim God exclusively for itself. Christian educational strategies that use processes of contextualization provide a way for respecting the heritages of every culture.

Contextual strategies honor the experiences of the learner, and the strategies recognize the importance of the culture in which the learner's experience takes place. Contextual strategies assume rapid change in the ecology and social environment and continuing change in the world community (an increased awareness of the interdependence of nations).

These changes are influenced largely by technology and economics. Technology and the world economy have provided the human community with many new opportunities and responsibilities. Responsibilities include attention that must be given to the possibility of destroying creation. The human community has the capability to extinguish itself. Destruction can come through nuclear warfare or through consumption of the earth's natural resources. These changes give occasion for humanity to understand anew its own identity.

Recognizing, understanding, and fashioning identity is central to contextual strategies of Christian education. Such strategies provide greater potential than either translation or adaptation because they begin with questions persons and communities raise themselves. Contextual strategies do not give theology's pre-existing answers to emerging concerns. Rather the data from the personal living document or the cultural text move toward the faith traditions. Contextual strategies assume that the particularity of individual cultures is significant. Contextual strategies allow for the stories and actions from within the culture to be voiced by persons who have shared a unique experience.

Christian education processes must provide strategies for attending to personal and group identity. Honoring the integrity of the experiences and heritages of every culture honors their identity. Christian education respects the experiences of African Americans when it recognizes their distinctive conditions of relationships within United States culture.

Educating for Change

Christian education that is located in understandings of God's immanence and transcendence makes Christian transformation possible. God's involvement is with the world so that the world, through Christ, may be changed. And for this purpose God acts as the Unmoved Mover. God is not swayed from having humanity and creation become one with the divine purpose and intent. In this regard, Grant L. Shockley wrote, "The challenge of religious education to Protestantism from a black perspective . . . emphasizes the Kingdom of God as the goal of the human community and the prophetic word as the conscience of the nation."[33]

Christian transformation is revolutionary. It includes an understanding of persons and communities who have been and are being changed radically and who are crushing existing world conditions and replacing them with God's community to come. According to Shockley, Christian education that is transformational works at "redefining discipleship in relation to: gospel and history; church and world; Christian faith and society. [It is] a break that goes so deep that the new state beyond it cannot be understood as the continuation of what went on before."[34]

Christian education that is located in views of God's immanence and transcendence advocates the cause of Christ. (See Parker J. Palmer, *To Know as We Are Known,* 1983.) Learning is not detached from daily living the life of Christian faith. Both teacher and learner are subject to the truth of Christ. When Christian education affirms that God extends beyond human knowledge, then knowledge is not used for manipulation and control. Instead, teachers teach and learners learn in order to be changed so that all may become subject to God's truth and promises known in Jesus Christ.

Christian education that is located in understandings of God's immanence and transcendence embraces personal and social responsibility at every phase of the process. Persons are invited to become engaged with the truth of Christ so that they may work on behalf of Christ. The transformative nature of Christian education, in the words of African-American culture, may be referred to as "the struggle."

Transformation is not an overnight-express experience. Old ways die hard. Change is a struggle. The African-American experience is an experience of struggle. The phrase, "the struggle," for African Americans summarizes the past, the present, and the promised yet unrealized future. From the experiences of struggle, African Americans have defined an approach to living, a way of being in and relating to the world. We fervently believe that greater, systemic change is coming even though it has come only in part over almost 400 years.

Attention must be given to struggle as a meaningful way of naming education for transformation. African-American Christians know that struggle has relevance for living on behalf of Christ in the world. We recognize that there are ideas and experiences that are worth wrestling with and for. Christian education that is transformative works to make a difference.

Christian education informs in order to transform. And the difference is not as vague as some persons contend. Continuity does exist amid the change and struggle. The continuity is provided in Jesus of Nazareth, the Christ of God. Transforming Christian education empowers persons and communities to align their will to the ways of Jesus Christ. It inspires persons with courage to commit themselves to live after Christ's example. It leads them into the world to witness on behalf of Christ through service to others.

Cultural integrity—respect for the traditions and experiences of African Americans—empowers the thinking, motivation, and action of African Americans. Christian education that has cultural integrity for African Americans will enhance African-American expressions of Christian responsibility and faith commitments. Teaching scripture with cultural integrity inspires African Americans to become faithful disciples of Christ and to witness to God's future community in this present world.

CHAPTER 6
TEACHING INSIGHTS FROM AFRICAN-AMERICAN CHURCHES

> For I handed on to you as of first importance what I in turn had received: that Christ died for our sins in accordance with the scriptures, and that he was buried, and that he was raised on the third day in accordance with the scriptures (1 Corinthians 15:3-4).

Teaching scripture in African-American congregations must be Christ-centered. Jesus, the Christ of God, is the centerpiece of both personal and communal salvation. Christ is the hope of history. At all times and in all places, teachers must point to God's unmerited favor extended to the human family by the merits of Jesus' life, death, and resurrection. Teachers must reveal that Christ is "the ground of hope and the promise of life from sin and death." Teaching scripture makes plain that God saves by the benefit of the blood of Christ.

Teaching scripture in African-American congregations makes known that Jesus Christ is Savior and that Jesus Christ is Lord. Teachers in African-American congregations teach so that learners may see and accept as Lord the Christ who saves. Teachers must live so that God's unmerited favor and grace is understood as free but not cheap. The cost of discipleship for the first followers of Christ was often persecution and death. How may Christians dare to teach and expect any response less than a life of sacrifice and servanthood? African-American Christian teachers must work to inspire learners with courage to trust in the God made known in Christ and to claim Christ as their Lord.

Teaching scripture in ways that claim Christ as Lord bears witness through a life of radical obedience. Teachers and learners must come to know the lordship of Christ in both its vertical and horizontal dimensions. Disciples who claim Christ as their Lord accept responsibility to represent Christ in the world. Teachers who assume Christ as the centerpiece of salvation perform acts of service in the world. Learners become the hands and feet of Jesus in society. Teaching scripture in African-American congregations confesses Jesus Christ as Savior and claims him as Lord.

Teaching scripture in African-American congregations must be community focused.

Rain does not fall on one roof alone.—Cameroonian proverb

Community is the core of the African-American experience, and community is an essential focus of the biblical witness as well. Community is at the core of both the African-American and Christian experiences because life is relational. The character of God is communal: God the Creator, God the Redeemer, and God the Sustainer of life.

Historically, in different ways and with different words, African Americans upheld the African view, "I am because we are; and because we are, therefore I am." This was the basis of the clan and tribe. This understanding was the basis for the survival of African slaves in the United States, too. Given the break-up of the African family during slavery, it is impossible to know who is related to whom. Therefore, African Americans must exhibit a life that is parallel to the quote above. All African Americans must be seen as sisters and brothers. Everyone is related one to another.

Teaching scripture and living the Word that is taught happen in the context of community. God acts in community. Teaching scripture as and for the community is vital to the life of the congregation. The acts of God are announced in community. The people of God, "the laos," as a community hear, understand, and are called to respond to God's Word. The church's history is a story about a community's obedient and disobedient responses to God's activity. God's movement in the world is authenticated in community.

African-American teachers must re-establish community for learners. And learners must discover the attitudes, understandings, and skills that are needed to sustain the communities established. When the scripture is faithfully taught, learners come to see themselves as their brother's and sister's keeper, as part of God's world community.

Teaching scripture in African-American congregations must claim the attention and allegiance of its leaders. "Leaders" here refers to pastors, church officers, and teachers. Learners are sustained in their study and discipleship by the commitment and enthusiasm of others. Leaders lead by example. Pastors, officers, and teachers must become disciplined learners, too. Leaders must show the way by doing as they say. Followers become convinced about the convictions of others when the convictions of others are consistent with their actions.

Pastors, church officers, and teachers demonstrate the importance of teaching and studying scripture by example. These examples are vital to the life and health of the congregation and each Christian disciple. Teachers in African-American congregations will not be as effective without the support of the pastor's and church officers' leadership.

The leadership and support of pastors and church officers may be given in the form of raising expectations, empowering others to service, or creating and sustaining an environment of study. Pastors, officers, and teachers may question and challenge personal and group patterns that do not bear witness to the markings of Christian discipleship. Begin to envision and describe for others what a learning disciple and teaching congregation are like.

Pastors, officers, and teachers can empower others to teach and learn. They do this by sharing knowledge with others, by encouraging persons interested in teaching and learning to take advantage of skills-training opportunities, and by providing for teachers and learners the resources needed to carry out their task with excellence. Teachers are empowered to teach and learners are equipped to learn the scripture when information, skills, and resources are combined to nurture the congregation of God with God's Word.

> Knowledge is like a garden; if it is not cultivated it
> cannot be harvested.—Guinean proverb[36]

Pastors, officers, and teachers can sustain a learning énvironment. The strategies, structures, and operations of the church must work for realization of the church's mission. Pastors, officers, and teachers can organize in ways that support the teaching and learning of scripture. Sunday school and Bible study classes are not the only times when God's Word may be heard, used, or obeyed. The scripture can become the basis for study, reflection, and service throughout the life of the congregation. These acts demonstrate the commitment the pastors, officers, and teachers have to the ministry of teaching the scripture.

Teaching the scripture in African-American congregations enables persons to recognize blessings of God. The blessings of teaching scripture are numerous. Giving attention to the teaching of scripture provides the congregation with a common language. Those who teach the scripture share with the people of God the memory of God's people. A teacher empowers the congregation with a common vision and equips Christians with resources of faith for living.

Teaching scripture provides the community with its language. Language helps to make community possible. This includes what persons say and what they do. Words such as *grace, holiness, righteousness,* and *peace* may be explored and their worth uncovered when scripture is taught to enable a person's participation in the family of Christians. Actions such as turning the other cheek, blessing those who persecute you, loving your enemies, and rejoicing in tribulations may be made known and valued in new ways; leading learners toward union with God's will.

Teaching scripture empowers the church to remember past actions of the God whom they seek to serve. Scripture holds the common memory of the Christian community of faith. The biblical narrative is the reservoir that recalls the journey of God's people and the faithfulness of God on the journey. For Christians, the Word of God is the repository of their ancestors' actions. It is the wellspring from which the congregation's sense of identity, purpose, and vision emerges.

Let those speak who have seen with their eyes.—Zairean proverb

"Where there is no vision, people perish." Teaching scripture honors God and serves God's people by giving voice to the vision of God. Teaching scripture makes it possible for the church to view reality from the eyes of God. Without scripture providing a common vision for God's people, congregations are left to wander into the future as aimless individuals. Teaching scripture binds persons one to another and all to the will of God. Teaching scripture offers believers resources of faith for the living of their days. The challenges of life do not allow persons to live solely on the faith of their ancestors. The questions of today remind persons that the road of choices for tomorrow has not been passed before. But the Word of God, with all its nourishing power, can empower persons to faithfully endure.

Teaching the scripture empowers persons to experience God's immanence, God's transcendence, and God's transformative presence and power. Key markings and events of life are renewed by the witness of biblical writers. Persons may come to value and evaluate previous life choices in new and different ways. They are inspired to faithfully respond to a new or changing situation with confidence and hope. Teaching scripture with cultural integrity enriches faith and encourages acts of increasing faithfulness.

Appendices 1 and 2 can assist pastors and educational leaders in understanding the importance and function of the Bible in the congregation. The surveys will help also in selecting strategies for particular audiences and needs. Permission is granted to adapt the Appendices and Surveys as needed in seminary or local church settings.

APPENDIX 1
SCRIPTURE STUDY SURVEY

1. In what settings should the scripture be taught and studied?

2. In what settings is the scripture taught and studied now? For example, Sunday school, Saturday ethnic school, choir rehearsal, administrative planning meetings, and so forth.

3. What is the ideal role of scripture for individual members of the congregation?

4. What is the ideal role of scripture for the congregation's boards, councils, and committees?

5. What is the ideal role of scripture in relation to the outreach and social action ministries of the congregation?

6. In your opinion, what are the reasons for studying the scripture? List in order of importance from one (highest) to four (lowest).

   (   ) To gain information and knowledge about what I am to become and do.
   (   ) To clarify and understand the ways of Christian discipleship.
   (   ) To experience nurture and inspiration for the day.
   (   ) To explore Christian responses to personal, political, economic, and cultural concerns.

7. What expectations, if any, do you have about the consequences of Bible study?

8. What are some actions you can take to encourage an increased study of scripture in the congregation?

9. Who are the persons who may be enlisted to assist in

increasing the study of scripture in the life of the congregation?

10. What commitments, information, skills training, and resources are needed to increase the study of scripture in the congregation?

APPENDIX 2
MISSION ORIENTATION SURVEY
OF YOUR CONGREGATION

Maintain an active evangelism program, inviting the unchurched to participate.	Cooperate with other religious groups for community improvements.
Encourage members to make explicit faith declarations to friends and neighbors.	Provide aid and services to people in need.
Reach out to members of other religious groups with the message of true salvation.	Help persons understand themselves as agents of God's love and hope.
Protect members from the false teachings of other religious groups.	Encourage members, as individuals, to be involved in social issues.
Prepare members for a world to come in which the cares of this world are absent.	Encourage members to reach their own decisions on matters of faith and morals.
Resist the temptation of contemporary "pleasures" and lifestyles.	Sponsor organized social action groups within the congregation.
Prepare members for a world to come in which the cares of this world are absent.	Promote social change through organized, collective influence.
Accept one's condition and status as controlled and determined by God.	Encourage the pastor to speak out on social and political issues.
Encourage obedience to civil laws as a religious duty.	Provide financial support for social action activities.
Foster a sense of patriotism as a religious duty.	Support corporate congregational participation in social and political issues.

1) Choose one of the four areas that best describes the mission emphasis of your congregation.

2) What are the opportunities, limitations, and responsibilities for studying the scripture as the congregation executes its mission?

Based on *Varieties of Religious Presence,* Roozen, McKinney, and Carroll (New York: The Pilgrim Press, 1984).

APPENDIX 3
AFRICAN-AMERICAN RESOURCES: A SAMPLE

The resources below can help tell and interpret the heritage of African Americans and supplement the strategy approaches to scripture.

CHILDREN'S RESOURCES

PIONEERING FAITH: Memories of Courage

Uncle Tom's Cabin, Harriet Beecher Stowe (Harper and Row, 1983)

Follow the Drinking Gourd, Jeanette Winter (Afred A. Knopf, Inc., 1988)

Jesse Jackson: A Voice for Change, Steven Atfinaski (Jeffrey Weiss Group, Inc., 1989)

If You Traveled on the Underground Railroad, Ellen Lenine (Scholastic, Inc., 1988)

Take a Walk in Thin Shoes, Glennette Tilley Turner (Cobblehill, 1989)

MEANINGFUL SUFFERING: Agents Against the Odds

Long Journey Home, Julius Lester (Scholastic, Inc., 1972)

To Be a Slave, Julius Lester (Scholastic, Inc., 1968)

Wilma Rudolph, Tom Biracree (Chelsea House, 1988)

Jackie Robinson, Jim O'Conner (Random House, 1989)

Freedom Train, Dorothy Sterling (Scholastic, Inc., 1954)

HISTORY-MAKING HOPE: Courage to Imagine, Courage to Become

Art, Poetry, Music

Rosa Parks, Eloise Greenfield (Crowell, 1973)

YOUTH RESOURCES

PIONEERING FAITH: Memories of Courage

From Slavery to Freedom, John Hope Franklin
Roots, Alex Haley (Doubleday, 1976)

Eyes on the Prize, Juan Williams, 1988; The Classic Slave Narrative, Heary Louis Gates, Jr. (Penguin, 1987)

Martin Luther King, Jr. and the Freedom Movement, Lillie Patters ("Facts on File," 1989)

MEANINGFUL SUFFERING: Agents Against the Odds

The Souls of Black Folk, W.E.B. Dubois (Bantam, 1989)

The Autobiography of an Ex-Colored Man, James Weldon Johnson, 1912 first printing, 1977 edition

HISTORY-MAKING HOPE: Courage to Imagine, Courage to Become

Black Folktales, Julius Lester (Grove Press, 1969)

Behind the Scenes, Elizabeth Kecldey (Oxford University Press, 1988)

Up from Slavery, Booker T. Washington (Penguin Books, 1986)

ADULTS

PIONEERING FAITH: Memories of Courage

Eyewitness: The Negro in American History, William Loren Katz (Belmont, CA: David S. Lake Publishers, 1974)

I Dream a World, Brian Lanker (Stewart Tabori and Change, 1989)

Forged in Battle, Joseph G. Glatthaar (Free Press, 1990)

Let the Trumpet Sound, Stephen B. Oates (Plumi, 1982)

MEANINGFUL SUFFERING: Agents Against the Odds

A History in Their Own Words: The Black Americans, Milton Miltzer (Harper and Row, 1984)

He Included Me, Louis Westling (University of Georgia Press, 1989)

HISTORY-MAKING HOPE: Courage to Imagine, Courage to Become

Parting the Waters, Taylor Branch (Touchstone, 1988)

Black Women Writers, Mari Evans (Doubleday, 1983)

Black Leaders of the Nineteenth Century, Litwack/Miur (University of Illinois, 1988)

TEACHER RESOURCES

A Common Destiny: Blacks and American Society, Gerald David Jaynes and Robin M. Williams, Jr., editors (Washington, D.C.: National Academy Press, 1989)

Countering the Conspiracy to Destroy Black Boys, Volume I, Jawanza Kunjufu (Chicago, IL: African-American Images, 1985)

Countering the Conspiracy to Destroy Black Boys, Volume II, Jawanza Kunjufu (Chicago, IL: African-American Images, 1986)

Developing Positive Self-Images and Discipline in Black Children, Jawanza Kunjufu (Chicago, IL: African-American Images, 1984)

Sing for Freedom: The Story of the Civil Rights Movement Through Its Songs, edited and compiled by Guy and Candie Carawan (Bethlehem, PA: Sing Out Publications, 1990)

Soul Theology: The Heart of American Black Culture, Henry H. Mitchell and Nicholas Cooper Lewter (San Francisco, CA: Harper and Row, 1986)

Troubling Biblical Waters: Race, Class, and Family, Cain Hope Felder (Maryknoll, NY: Orbis Books, 1989)

Working with Black Youth, Charles R. Foster and Grant S. Shockley (Nashville: Abingdon, 1989)

ENDNOTES

Introduction

1. Paul Laurence Dunbar, *Complete Poems of Paul Laurence Dunbar* (New York: Dodd, Mead & Co., 1913).
2. "Meaning-making"—One view of meaning involves the signifying of a person's intent. Meaning-making is concerned with transfer of information from memory to active conscience with an intent to possess and apply information in life situations. The routine patterns of persons' lives are filled with meaning—what they intend to think and do in life. Their actions and behaviors are the signature of their intent.
3. Marianne Sawicki, "Historical Methods and Religious Education," in *Religious Education,* Vol. 82, No. 3, (Summer 1987), p. 376. Used by permission.
4. Jack L. Seymour, "Power and History: History as 'Critical' Analysis, in *Religious Education,* Vol. 82, No. 3, (Summer 1987), p. 350. Used by permission.
5. "The Story Strategy" is a metaphor. Like all metaphors it is used with the intent to "carry over" or transfer ideas and understandings from one place to another. In recent years many Christian theologians and educators have used and continue to use the metaphor of story to convey God's activity in creation and the response of persons. The uniqueness of the story metaphor for African Americans emerges from and is shaped by their particular historical/cultural experience.

Chapter 1

6. John N. Paden and Edward W. Soja, *The African Experience* (Evanston, IL: Northwestern University Press, 1970). Reprinted by permission of Northwestern University Press.
7. C.H. Johnson, ed., *God Struck Me Dead: Religious Conversion Experiences and Autobiographies of Ex-Slaves* (New York: United Church Press, 1969), pp. 15-18. Copyright © 1969 United Church Press. Reprinted with permission.
8. "Living human document" is here used as presented by Anton Boisen and discussed by Charles V. Gerkin in *The Living Human Document* (Nashville: Abingdon Press, 1984), pp. 37-54. Personal stories and persons' perception of their stories are important. These stories, viewed as religious struggles, must be understood in concrete daily relationships and circumstances. Humans are living texts to be upheld and understood, just as the scripture is approached for meaning and understanding.
9. David Feinstein and Stanley Krippner, *Personal Mythology: The Psychology of Your Evolving Self* (St. Martin's Press, 1988), pp. 35, 24.

Chapter 2

10. C. Ellis Nelson, *Where Faith Begins* (Richmond, VA: John Knox Press, 1976), pp. 10, 186.
11. Copyright © 1926 by Alfred A. Knopf, Inc. and renewed 1954 by Langston

Hughes. Reprinted from *Selected Poems of Langston Hughes* by permission of Alfred A. Knopf, Inc.

12. Turnbull, in Paden and Soja, pp. 48ff.
13. Martin Luther King, Jr., *Strength to Love* (Philadephia: Augsburg Fortress Publishers, 1981), p. 110. Used by permission.
14. Wilfred Cantwell Smith, *Faith and Belief,* p. 37. Copyright © 1979 by Wilfred Cantwell Smith. Published by Princeton University Press. Used by permission.
15. Ibid., pp. 12-13.
16. Paden and Soja, p. 5.

Chapter 3

17. Bishop Joseph A. Johnson, Jr., *The Soul of the Black Preacher* (New York: United Church Press, 1971), pp. 149-150. Used by permission as published.
18. Ibid, p. 151.
19. Alex Haley, *Roots* (New York: Doubleday and Company, 1975), p. 3. Used by permission.

Chapter 4

20. Excerpts from C. Eric Lincoln, *Race, Religion, and the Continuing American Dilemma.* Copyright © 1984 by C. Eric Lincoln. Reprinted by permission of Hill and Wang, a division of Farrar, Straus and Giroux, Inc.
21. Religious Education Press, Inc., Birmingham, Ala. *Does the Church Really Want Religious Education?* edited by Marlene Mayr—"From Emancipation to Transformation to Consummation" by Grant S. Shockley (chapter contributor). Used by permission.
22. Lincoln, p. 104.

Chapter 5

23. Shockley, pp. 221-228.
24. Jack L. Seymour, *From Sunday School to Church School* (New York: University Press of America, 1982), p. 29.
25. The word *translation* is commonly used in reference to versions of the Bible. However, the term is used here with reference to a particular approach to discovering meaning(s) of biblical texts.
26. H. Richard Niebuhr, *The Social Sources of Denominationalism* (New York: Henry Holt & Co., 1957), pp. 3, 264-265.
27. Edward B. Taylor, *Primitive Culture, Vol. I* (New York: Harper & Row Publishers, 1958), p. 1.
28. Michael Apple, *Teachers and Texts* (New York: Routledge & Kegan Paul, 1986), pp. 84ff. Reprinted from *Teachers and Texts* with the permission of the publisher, Routledge, Chapman & Hall.
29. Wade W. Nobles, "African Philosophy: Foundations for Black Psychology," in *Black Psychology,* ed. by Reginald L. Jones (1980), p. 32. Used by permission.
30. Janice E. Hale-Benson, *Black Children: Their Roots, Culture, and Learning*

Styles, revised edition. (Baltimore/London: The Johns Hopkins University Press, 1986), p. 12. Used by permission.

31. Africans Americans . . . who are in the more privileged sectors of the society have more access to the cultural resources of the dominant group, and the retentions are less pure. . . . Black and Spanish ethnicity do not seem to correlate well with upper-middle-class lifestyle. Therefore, ethnicity has less influence on the behavior of middle-class Blacks and Americans of Spanish origin. On the other hand, the influence of ethnicity is stronger than social class influences among the lower classes of those groups. (Hale-Benson, pp. 15, 27)

32. James Weldon Johnson, "Lift Every Voice and Sing." Copyright © 1921 Edward B. Marks Music Co. Used by permission.

33. Shockley, p. 230.

34. Ibid, p. 232.

Chapter 6

35. Charlotte and Wolf Leslau, *African Proverbs* (White Plains, N.Y.: Peter Pauper Press, 1985), p. 15.

36. Ibid., p. 31.

37. Ibid., p. 18.

BIBLIOGRAPHY

Achtemeier, Paul J., editor. *Harper's Bible Dictionary.* San Francisco, CA: Harper & Row, Publishers, 1985.

Apple, Michael. *Teachers & Texts: A Political Economy of Class and Gender Relations in Education.* New York & London: Routledge Chapman & Hall, 1988.

Barnes, Edward J. "The Black Community as the Source of Positive Self-Concept for Black Children: A Theoretical Perspective," in *Black Psychology,* Reginald L. Jones, ed. New York: Harper and Row, 1980, pp. 106-130.

Bennis, Warren. *Why Leaders Can't Lead.* San Francisco, CA: Jossey-Bass Publishers, 1989.

Birchett, Colleen. "A History of Religious Education in the Black Church," in *Urban Church Education.* Birmingham, AL: Religious Education Press, 1989.

Bryant, David J. *Faith and the Play of Imagination.* Macon, GA: Mercer University Press, 1989.

Buttrick, George Arthur, general editor. *The Interpreter's Dictionary of the Bible,* Vols 1-4. Nashville, TN: Abingdon Press, 1962.

Chestang, Leon W. *Character Development in a Hostile Environment.* Chicago, IL: University of Chicago Press, 1972.

Cobb, John B. Jr., and David Ray Griffin. *Process Theology: An Introductory Exposition.* Philadelphia, PA: The Westminster Press, 1976.

Cross, William E., Jr. "Models of Psychological Nigrescence: A Literature Review," in *Black Psychology,* Reginald L. Jones, ed. New York: Harper and Row, 1980, pp. 81-98.

Edmonds, Billingsley, et al. "A Black Response to Christopher Jenck's Inequality and Certain Other Issues," *Black Psychology,* Reginald L. Jones, ed. New York: Harper and Row, 1980, pp. 244-255.

Feinstein, David, and Stanley Krippner. *Personal Mythology: The Psychology of Your Evolving Self.* New York: St. Martin's Press (J. P. Tarcher), 1988.

Foster, Charles R. *Teaching in the Community of Faith.* Nashville, TN: Abingdon Press, 1982.

_____, and Grant S. Shockley. *Working with Black Youth*. Nashville, TN: Abingdon Press, 1989.

Fowler, James W. *Becoming Adult, Becoming Christian: Adult Development and Christian Faith*. New York: Harper & Row, Publishers, 1984.

Gerkin, Charles V. *The Living Human Document: Revisioning Pastoral Counseling in a Hermeneutical Mode*. Nashville, TN: Abingdon Press, 1984.

_____, *Widening the Horizons: Pastoral Responses to a Fragmented Society*. Philadelphia, PA: Westminster Press, 1986.

Groome, Thomas H. *Christian Religious Education: Sharing Our Story and Vision*. New York: Harper & Row, Publishers, 1982.

Hale-Benson, Janice E. *Black Children: Their Roots, Culture, and Learning Styles*. Johns Hopkins, 1986.

Haley, Alex. *Roots*. Garden City, NJ: Doubleday, 1976.

Hanson, Grant W. *Foundations for the Teaching Church*. Valley Forge, PA: Judson Press, 1986.

Harding, Vincent. *The Acts of God and the Children of Africa*. Philadelphia, PA: United Church Press, 1973.

Hessel, Dieter T. "A Whole Ministry of (Social) Education," in *Religious Education Journal*, Vol. 78, Number 4, Fall 1983.

Holland, Joe, and Peter Henriot, S.J. *Social Analysis: Linking Faith and Justice*. Orbis Books, 1983.

Jones, James M. *New Roads to Faith: Black Perspectives in Christian Education: Educating People for Liberation and Collective Growth*. Philadelphia, PA: United Church Press, 1973.

Jones, Reginald L., editor. *Black Psychology*. New York: Harper & Row, Publishers, 1980.

Jones, Robert E. "Learning to Face Diversity in Urban Churches," in *Urban Church Education*. Birmingham, AL: Religious Education Press, 1989.

Kennedy, William B. "Pursuing Justice and Peace: Challenge to Religious Educators," in *Religious Education Journal*, Vol. 78, Number 4, Fall 1983.

King, Martin Luther, Jr. *Strength to Love*. Philadelphia, PA: Fortress Press, 1981.

Klatib, S.M. "Black Studies and the Study of Black People: Reflections on the Distinctive Characteristics of Black Psychology," in *Black Psychology*, Reginald L. Jones, ed. New York: Harper and Row, 1980, pp. 48-55.

Kochman, Thomas. *Black and White Styles in Conflict.* Chicago: University of Chicago Press, 1983.

Kouzes, James M., and Barry Z. Posner. *The Leadership Challenge: How to Get Extraordinary Things Done in Organizations.* San Francisco, CA: Jossey-Bass Publishers, 1987.

Leslau, Charlotte and Wolf. *African Proverbs.* White Plains, NY: Peter Pauper Press, Inc. 1985.

Lincoln, C. Eric. *The Negro Pilgrimage in America.* New York: Bantam Books, Inc., 1984.

_____. *Race, Religion, and the Continuing American Dilemma.* London: Collins Publishers, 1984.

Lincoln, Yvonna S., and Egon G. Guba. *Naturalistic Inquiry.* Newbury Park, CA: Sage Publications, 1985.

Maas, Robin. *The Church Bible Study Handbook.* Nashville, TN: Abingdon Press, 1982.

Martin, George. *Reading Scripture As the Word of God.* Ann Arbor, MI: Servant Books, 1982.

Mitchell, Henry H., and Cooper-Lewter, Nicholas C. *Soul Theology: The Heart of American Black Culture.* San Francisco, CA: Harper & Row, Publishers, 1986.

Mulholland, M. Robert, Jr. *Shaped by the Word.* Nashville, TN: The Upper Room, 1985.

Nichols, Paul. "Blacks and the Religious Education Movement," in *Changing Patterns of Religious Education.* Nashville, TN: Abingdon Press, 1984.

Niebuhr, H. Richard. *The Social Sources of Denominationalism.* Magnolia, MA: Peter Smith, 1984.

Nobles, Wade W. "African Philosophy: Foundations for Black Psychology," in *Black Psychology*, Reginald L. Jones, ed. New York: Harper and Row, 1980, pp. 23-36.

_____, "Extended Self: Rethinking the So-Called Negro Self-Concept," in *Black Psychology*, Reginald L. Jones, ed. New York: Harper and Row, 1980.

Paden, John N., and Soja, Edward W. *The African Experience, Vol. 3B.* Evanston, IL: Northwestern University Press, 1970.

Palmer, Parker J. *To Know As We Are Known: A Spirituality of Education.* New York: Harper & Row, Publishers, 1983.

Pobee, John S. *Toward an African Theology.* Nashville, TN: Abingdon Press, 1979.

Rogers, Donald B., ed. *Urban Church Education.* Birmingham, AL: Religious Education Press, 1989.

Roozen, William, and Carroll. *Varieties of Religious Presence: Mission in Public Life.* New York: Pilgrim Press, 1984.

Sawicki, Marianne. "Historical Methods and Religious Education," in *Religious Education Journal,* Vol. 82, Number 3, Summer 1987.

Schein, Edgar H. *Process Consultation, Vol. II: Lessons for Managers and Consultants.* Reading, MA: Addison-Wesley Publishing Company, Inc., 1988.

Schreiter, Robert J. *Constructing Local Theologies.* Mary Knolls, NY: Orbis Books, 1985.

Seymour, Jack L. *From Sunday School to Church School: Communities in Protestant Church Education in the United States.* New York: University Press of America, 1982.

———, and Donald E. Miller. *Contemporary Approaches to Christian Education.* Nashville, TN: Abingdon Press, 1982.

———, "Power and History: History as 'Critical' Analysis," in *Religious Education Journal,* Vol. 82, Number 3, Summer 1987.

Shockley, Grant S., et al. *Christian Education Journey of Black Americans.* Nashville, TN: Discipleship Resources, 1985.

———, "From Emancipation to Transformation to Consumation," in *Does the Church Really Want Religious Education?* Marlene Mayr, editor. Birmingham, AL: Religious Education Press, 1988.

———, "Christian Education and the Black Religious Experience," in *Ethnicity in the Education of the Church.* Nashville, TN: Scarritt Press, 1987.

———, "Liberation Theology, Black Theology, and Religious Education," in *Foundations for Christian Education in an Era of Change.* Nashville, TN: Abingdon Press, 1976.

Snyder, Ross. *On Becoming Human.* Nashville, TN: Abington Press, 1967.

Stokes, Olivia P. *The Educational Role of Black Churches in the 70's and 80's.* Philadelphia, PA: United Church Press, 1973.

Streng, Frederick Jr., Charles L. Lloyd, Jr., et al. *Ways of Being Religious.* Englewood Cliffs, NJ: Prentice-Hall, Inc., 1973.

Tylor, Sir Edward B. *Primitive Culture, Vol. I.* New York: Harper & Row, 1958, p. 1.

Warford, Malcolm L. *The Necessary Illusion.* Philadelphia, PA: United Church Press, 1976.

Watley, William D. *Roots of Resistance: The Nonviolent Ethic of Martin Luther King, Jr.* Valley Forge, PA: Judson Press, 1985.

Wimberly, Edward P. and Anne Streaty. *Liberation and Human Wholeness: The Conversion Experiences of Black People in Slavery and Freedom.* Nashville, TN: Abingdon Press, 1986.

Wilson, William Julius. *The Declining Significance of Race: Blacks and Changing American Institutions.* Chicago: University of Chicago Press, 1980.